# SONGS AND STORIES

# OF

# A DIGGER'S SON

## BY

### JOHN WELDON EVANS

Copyright © 2008 by TJMF Publishing

Printed and Bound in the United States By
Publisher's Graphics, LLC

Cover Design by Jim Furber

Illustrations and Photos Courtesy of the
National Archives

ISBN Number: 9801003-1-3
13 digit ISBN Number: 978-0-9801003-1-0
Library of Congress Number: 2008907287


TJMF Publishing

# Dedication

In memory of my parents,

Cornelius Richard Evans
and
Marie Philomene Noel-Evans

V

## Introduction

La Boca was one of several segregated towns on the Panama Canal Zone for West Indians and other non-white, non-U.S.workers employed by the U.S.government to work on the Panama Canal. American citizens lived in separate, more comfortable, all-white communities built for U.S. citizens who were carefully selected in the southern district of the U.S. before they were employed to work on the Canal Zone. This was the Panama Canal Zone system, separate but unequal, which existed and was strictly enforced at that time; but I am not going to elaborate any further on the system, since my focus is on my birthplace, La Boca Town.

Historically, the town of La Boca was officially built in 1913, just before the ship S.S. Ancon made the first official transit of the Panama Canal, when Colonel Goethals (Chief Canal Engineer and later, first governor of the C.Z.) authorized its construction to provide accommodations for West Indian workers. The land was located southeast of Sosa Hill and north of the Pacific entrance to the Panama Canal. It was almost rectangular, bordered by four principal streets, Martinique Street, Santo Domingo Street, Gold Street (also known as Trinidad Street) and La Boca Road. At the northwest corner, on Martinique Street, was a commissary that supplied all hard goods, groceries, cold storage goods and canned foods. A school building stood at the south end overlooking the Pacific Ocean, and a clubhouse near the school. The clubhouse was later expanded to include a theatre built during World War II. An emergency fire station and a civilian defense headquarters were also built during the war. On the east side of town, a ball park was built between the houses and a field of huge oil storage tanks fenced off from the town. There was a park running through the center of town lengthwise on a narrow island bordered by Jamaica Prado, which went north on one side and south on the other side of the island. In the early days, up until 1941, there was a tram car that ran on rails along La

1

Boca Road and went into Panama City. There was a restaurant at the northwest end across La Boca Road that was later enlarged to service mostly bachelors who lived in the quarters. The town had one dispensary for first aid service only. La Boca grew from a town of several hundred residents at its inception in 1913 to over 6,000 by 1942 when more and more West Indians and other nationalities were assigned quarters there by the Canal Zone housing division. Many of the new residents were probably moved from towns inundated by the canal waterway.

La Boca was a great town for sports. On the ball ground, cricket was a favorite, also soccer, baseball, softball, and of course, track and field which provided a great deal of excitement for the residents. Divisional leagues and worker leagues competed there, playing baseball and softball for trophies. The West Indian cricket players in clean-cut white uniforms displayed fine skills hitting the cricket ball about, and on a muddy day soccer teams tussled up and down field kicking a soccer ball from one goal to the next. Many intramural track and field meets were held there; a number of fine athletes who trained there went on to compete in the 1938, 1946 and 1950 Pan-American Games and did very well.

But the life and history of the town was to be short-lived as there were forces, inevitable perhaps, that conspired against its existence. There were issues of politics, local struggles for nationalism, and what to do about all these transplanted people from the West Indies whose children and grandchildren had no permanent homes. Without developing these themes here, however, I will say only a few words about the influence of one group in particular that played a large part in the practice of discrimination on the Canal Zone and that had a hand in the early demise of La Boca. I am referring to the U.S. Metal Trade Council. They were the strongest pro-U.S., pro-white group on the Canal Zone at the time, with a strong lobbying influence both in the U.S. and on

2

the Canal Zone. For many years, they sought to acquire—for American citizens only—the land where La Boca was built. The governor resisted them in the early years, but in the late fifties and sixties, they succeeded in having all the West Indians moved out. It is important to mention here that on the Panama Canal Zone, all real property was owned by the Canal Zone government, and they could put residents out whenever they chose, which is what they did in the sixties to the residents of La Boca Town when the government either evicted them or relocated them to other non-U.S. towns in order to rebuild La Boca into a plush residential community for U.S. naval personnel.

Of course the irony is that, with the Carter-Torrijos Treaty in place, in the year 1999 when the canal was turned over to Panama, so were the Canal Zone towns, and most if not all American citizens had to repatriate back to the U.S. In any case, this did not help the West Indians who had lived on the Canal Zone, since, through no fault of theirs, they had no rights of ownership, no rights given them by law, no U.S. citizenship nor Panamanian citizenship during that time, no claims the two powers would respect, no protection under any country's laws, no recourse, so in fact, long before 1999 they were forced to leave what were once their homes for many years. Thus, inevitably, La Boca, C. Z. as we once knew it simply disappeared from the face of the earth. Here, then, is my story of the La Boca I knew when I was growing up.

Growing up in La Boca, Canal Zone, gave me the opportunity to see and know men and women who worked on the Panama Canal during and after its construction, including my father who was born in Gorgona, Canal Zone, one of the many pre-construction towns that today are under water. The Panama Canal had long been built by the time I was born, but in the thirties and forties as a young boy, I was able to listen to the stories of surviving diggers and canal workers. They were not much different from the stories of the three diggers I have written

3

about in Part II—Messrs. Leslie, Thompson, and Gallimore. It is well known that these African-Caribbean workers were exploited, mistreated, and underpaid under the system of the Canal Zone in the early 1900s, which was an extension of the prevailing racial policies in the United States at the time. Panamanians of African descent bore the brunt of discrimination and racism brought to the isthmus by the United States canal enterprise.

As a boy growing up in the Canal Zone, I always felt like two persons—one who was too busy living life to care, and another who was witnessing it, if you can imagine being in a play and observing it at the same time. As a witness, I couldn't understand (until much later) half of what was going on politically, but I knew that something didn't seem right when, as a boy, I couldn't walk through certain (white) neighborhoods without being arrested for loitering, or when I couldn't pick a mango off the ground that fell off a tree that nobody wanted without being arrested or treated like a thief. It seemed to me it was better to fill my belly than to let it rot on the ground. I couldn't understand either why we had to live in segregated parts of the Canal Zone, and why our sections didn't look as fancy with fine brick buildings and lawns, like the white sections with fewer families living in them. I couldn't understand why we had to shop in a different store, eat in a different restaurant, or go to a different clubhouse, movie theatre, or school. I didn't understand why the places where we lived and shopped were called *silver* and the places white people lived and shopped were called *gold* and why the water fountains and the toilets were labeled *silver* and *gold* and we couldn't use the gold service or drink the gold water. As a boy, I knew all of this was wrong—at least the witness in me knew—but I did what everybody else did—made the best of the situation and went about living anyway. I personally didn't let discrimination bother me too much then—at least the person in me who was living and enjoying nature and making the most of life didn't let it bother him. The other person, the witness,

4

was more serious and quiet most of the time, because I pushed him aside until I was much older.

Our parents came to the isthmus with no illusions. They were aware of the system, its codes and taboos, and they abhorred them deeply, but could do little to change them at the time—it would be for another generation to take up the struggle. Our parents did, however, persevere in spite of the barriers and in their own way still kept their heads high. Without exception, each and every Caribbean community on the Panama Canal Zone, such as La Boca, Red Tank, Paraiso, Gamboa, and Silver City, exemplified the life and quality of a proud, unselfish, courageous and hardworking people, who instilled in their children high moral values as well as a spiritual foundation, and encouraged their offspring to strive for a better life than they had.

In the writings presented in this book, I did not devote my poems and stories for the most part to racism on the Canal Zone and the evils it represented. Instead, I spent most, if not all, of my energies writing about the people I knew and of events that took place in our everyday community life, for, no matter how segregated and discriminatory the Canal Zone system was, within each *silver* community, daily human activities went on with all of the color, drama, humor, triumphs and pain that accompanied them. I preferred to write about such things, which had more meaning in my life.

These poems and stories, therefore, are my reflections about people, places and events that were part of my Panama Canal Zone experiences. Poetry is a form that I like to use as in Part I, for it sometimes enables me to connect more personally to the subjects, places and events. These poems and stories in a special way represent a nostalgia that comes over me from time to time for a past and a place that are gone forever, except in memory.

5

# PART I : SONGS

## The Digger's Sonnet

O valiant men of sinews dark and strong,
who toiled on cragged hills and treacherous slopes
far from your native lands, what dreams and hopes
sustained you and helped ease the parching sun?
Was it for loved ones that you dared to come
so far to toil on these hills and these slopes?
You could not know the great impact your strokes
would make collectively as your arms raised and swung,
digging and moving tons of earth each day!
Would that I could return through time to tell
and show you all the things that since have been
because you left your homelands far away
and braved a jungle and moved earth until
a great man-made canal came into being!

This poem is dedicated to the Caribbean workers whose labor contributed to the building of the Panama Canal.

### Diggers of the Big Ditch

O Tell the world, brave Caribbeans,
how the great *Big Ditch* was built;
how from jungles, hills, and swamplands
rose that man-made waterway;
how you sailed across an ocean
from your homelands far away
to a land made great and prosperous
by your sacrifices there—
without you there'd be no water
in the great *Big Ditch* today!

O Tell the world, brave Caribbeans,
how you proved your fortitude
when others tried and failed;
how you stood up proud and strong,
excavating, building dams,
clearing swamplands, building railways,
pouring concrete down the lines;
how your backs strained from hard labor
in the gullies, on the slopes;
how you toiled in rain, in grime,
and in insect-infested swamps;
how you fell in mortal agony
in the fields from day to day
on contractor's perilous slopes,
in Culebra Cut, in Gaillard Straights,
crushed by landslides, dynamite,
and by heavy falling rocks,
struck by typhoid, dysentery,
malaria, *yellow jack!*

O Tell the world, Afro-Antilleans,
how you toiled sunup till sundown
for a measly rate of pay;
tell them how you lived in Jim Crow,
segregated *silver* towns,
how you drank from *silver* fountains,

9

washed in *silver* bathhouses,
dropped your *silver* wastes in public,
*silver* shacks or outhouses,
how you shopped for goods in *silver*
Jim Crow commissaries!

O Tell the world, brave Caribbeans,
how the great Big Ditch was built;
how your rich blood, sweat and tears
drenched a land not of your birth!
And tell about the years spent,
after the Ditch was built,
laboring long hours on the dredges,
loading cargo on the piers,
forging steel in metal shops,
making nuts and bolts and parts,
welding metal plates with torches,
driving rivets into hulls,
laboring on the P.C. railroad,
in the yards or on the trains,
laying pipelines, building scaffolds,
raising miles of 'lectric poles,
working hard as carpenter,
electrician, plumber, helper,
quarry man, bricklayer, mechanic,
chauffeur, sanitation man,
clerk, teacher, painter, policeman,
office worker, janitor,
working hard as field laborer
or grave digger in graveyards!

O Tell the world, Afro-Antilleans,
how you worked on the Canal Zone
but you had no voice or vote,
could not influence those who governed
whether they were right or wrong,
and when all your strength was gone,
from the weight of all those years,
how they cast you off with no pension
like old and worn-out shoes!

O Tell the world, brave Caribbeans,
what no history books have told:

how you lived and prayed and hoped;
how you raised your families;
how you brought forth generations
and gave them a legacy,
not of gold and fancy titles,
not of empty labels, no,
but a legacy of fortitude
written in sweat and blood and tears—
a legacy of courage,
of wisdom, songs, and hope,
a legacy of pride and of undying faith.

Yes, be proud, Afro Caribbeans,
wherever you may be,
for you left your native islands
and went forth to dig a ditch
and enriched a land that was all
swamp and jungle when you came,
for you showed when others failed
how much you could endure,
and helped build the greatest waterway
by man with sweat and blood,
and you taught your sons and daughters,
who then taught their sons and daughters...
Now the heritage that you gave
is endowed within their seeds!
It is far richer than honors
never given to your name!

The Caribbean workers whose labor helped dig the Panama Canal were mistreated, underpaid and unappreciated. After they gave a lifetime of hard labor, if they survived till then, they were let go when they were disabled or too old to work. Many of them were shipped back home with nothing to show for the years of sacrifice and service. When the ex-worker was on the boat, he was given $25 for himself, $25 for his wife and $10 for each child up to five children, and with that the U.S. Canal Zone government washed their hands of him. In 1937 after a congressional investigation took place, the U.S. Congress passed the Cash Disability Relief Act, which provided the terminated worker an old-age disability of $1 for each year of service up to a maximum of $25 per month, from which was deducted varied amounts depending on how much furniture they had in their homes, or how much savings they had. Sometimes it amounted to zero. I know of at least one respected school teacher who got nothing because over the fifty years he worked for the Panama Canal Zone government, he managed to sacrifice and save $10,000. They said he was too rich!

The following sonnet is about a disabled Panama Canal digger who was unable to work after more than forty years of service. His name is Herman Thompson, who is probably dead by now, but whom I had the privilege of visiting in 1982 in Washapali and who, to me, symbolizes the fate of many old-timers.

## The Old-Timer

I saw him there looking feeble and cold,
a remnant of what once was called a man,
cuddled 'neath sheets, straining to raise his hand
to greet me as I entered his abode:
a dark and dusty room with pieces old—
one broken chair, stove, table and "washpan!"
He could not walk; he could not even stand.
His weary eyes and voice both touched my soul.

Here was a man who once was proud and strong,
whose sweat and blood helped build a great canal
from which nations have prospered—but not he.
How was he thanked when all his strength was gone?
Not even a paltry pension for it all,
but left to die there in obscurity.

During the early years of the construction of the Panama Canal, 1904-1914, equal rights for women were unheard of, and finding work was almost impossible for them; but at least one woman I knew, Hannah, solved that problem when she impersonated a man and was shipped from the West Indies to work as a digger on the Canal. My parents knew her well as she often visited our home in La Boca, C.Z. She smoked a pipe and could spin a yarn or two!

## Hannah from Barbados

Brave Hannah sleeping in your grave,
your wages earned, your labor done,
when you were young, fearless and brave
how you strove hard beneath the sun

to prove yourself, to hold your own,
to walk with pride in this harsh world!
'Twas with no quarter gained nor shown
that you dared take on as a girl

the challenge of a man's world
way back in nineteen hundred seven,
when equal rights were still absurd
and sexist codes unjust to women!

You watched as men and boys shipped off
in boatloads from Barbados shore
to work in Panama, and scoffed
when they rejected you once more:

*Go home,* they said, *this is man's work!*
But you would never understand!
Why didn't they see despite a skirt
you could work just like any man?

Moreover, without work, living
was hard and you were very poor.
So when the next steamship came in,
you stood again on Bridegtown shore;

this time no more long skirt or hair,
you donned a man's garb, hat and shirt,
transformed yourself, devil may care,
into a digger ready to work!

How they were fooled! How they were conned
and did not pierce your masquerade!
They let you board the ship Ancon
under contract, and you were paid

real wages on the Pan Canal
for man's work in that jungle land.
You went and triumphed despite all,
and moved dirt, too, like any man!

Later you changed your role again
and donned a woman's skirt with pride;
you showed you could survive and then
you wed and raised children besides.

O what a rich and glorious story
you must have told your children who
can thank your daring destiny—
they have a past and future too!

Your courage is an inspiration.
Hats off to you, brave Hannah, who
scored one for women's liberation
a long, long time ago! Adieu!

A poem dedicated to the many women who made sacrifices during and after the construction of the Panama Canal, and who were the anchor of the family structure and the real heroes, in my opinion.

## I Sing

I sing of unsung heroines,
unsung, forgotten heroines
of yesterday,
who in the fullness of their youth
came to a land called Panama
and brought with them their dreams and hopes!

I sing of women pioneers,
all but forgotten pioneers
of yesterday,
who overcame adversity
with quiet strength and dignity –
such is their precious legacy!

I sing of unsung matriarchs,
keepers and teachers of the faith,
healers, martyrs,
brilliant self-made economists,
miracle workers, philosophers,
school teachers, midwives, homemakers!

I sing of women blessed with courage,
possessors of unfailing wisdom,
pillars of strength,
bravers of many challenges,
crusaders, humanitarians,
peacemakers, organizers!

I sing of nation builders,
shapers of countless destinies
for years to come,
guardians of hope, champions of love,
molders of character, children inspirers,
value instillers, spiritual sustainers!

I sing of unsung heroines,
women singing songs of hope
despite their pain,
women laughing, toiling, suffering, crying,
women mourning for lost loved ones
and bravely carrying on after them!

I sing of unsung heroines,
women caring, answering the calls,
faithfully,
of sick neighbors and friends in need,
women active in the churches,
women praying and doing for others!

I sing of unsung heroines
who did not build the Great Canal
across the Isthmus,
but who built the fabric that sustained
the brave diggers of the Canal!
(Some gave the world sons who were diggers!)

I sing of unsung heroines,
co-architects of that foundation
which they have given
to all the lives they touched and nurtured,
and in so doing engendered with
a special, and eternal flame!

Throughout the years, and even now,
who has but felt their warmth and glow
and could not sing
for these forgotten heroines,
knowing the melody we sing
is of ourselves? And so, I sing!

During one phase or another of the construction of the Panama Canal, workers of different nationalities were sometimes thrown together on the construction line. Whenever this happened, they had to find a way to communicate with each other, and most of the times they did; however, occasionally a language problem arose, such as the one in this poem:

### Poco Mas Arriba

When they were building the Canal,
Somewhere along the lines
A strange work crew was put together
Whose job was laying pipelines.

One of the men, a Spanish man,
couldn't speak a word of English;
the other two, a Bajan and
a Gringo, couldn't speak Spanish.

A *Spic* from Spain or Hispaniola,
a *Bajan* and a *Gringo*,
all three from different cultures and
couldn't speak each other's lingo.

Anyway, one day working one end
of a pipe, Spic had a problem:
Gringo was at the other end,
and Spic called out to him,

*"Arriba! Poco mas arriba!"*
*(Higher! Raise the pipe higher!)*
You see, the pipe was heavy, and
the Spic began to tire.

At first the Gringo looked bemused
But did not say a word!
the Spic thought, *Something's wrong with Gringo;*
*or else he never heard!*

So Spic called out again louder,
*Arriba! Poco mas arriba!*
The Gringo turned to Bajee then,
and Bajee said, *Wa's mattah!*

Said Gringo, *That damn Spic's shouting*
*some funny words at me!*
*You look like you know what he's saying,*
*tell me in English, Bajee!*

*It ain' none o' moi concerns wotevah,*
said Bajee, *but dis wa de pana seh,*
*'Go poke yoh mass in a rivah!'*
*That's what I thought he said,*

retorted Gringo, *and what's more,*
*he says it one more time*
*I'm going to let him have it for sure!*
Not knowing of his crime

poor Spic called out, *Poco mas arriba!*
What happened was a sin!
Before you could say, *hmmm*, Gringo
gave Spic one cross the chin!

*Take that! Poke your behind in the river!*
The Spic couldn't win, it was a pity!
He got so mad he quit; but Gringo
was barred from Panama City!

19

Commuting via the Panama Canal railroad between Colon and Panama City was a common thing in the early and mid 1900s for people who lived on either the Pacific or Atlantic side but worked on the opposite shore of the canal. It was also a popular means of travel when there were excursions to the Atlantic or Pacific sides to attend dances or to see prize fights, etc., or whenever people visited friends and relatives on either shore. It was either the railroad or the Highway, which was not always the safest route. Although the trains were well maintained, they were not air conditioned in those days, and the windows were kept open most of the time. The journey was usually relaxing and picturesque to most travelers.

## On a Locomotive from Colon to Panama City in 1951

Hear the whistle echo shrilly,
see the sparks begin to fly,
feel the tempo heighten quickly
as the engine rumbles by,

screeching, hissing, fuming, fussing,
wheeing, fleeing against time,
stirring, whirring, forging, fighting,
racing with a reckless rhyme:

Got to get there, can't be last,
not a moment must be lost;
got to get there very fast,
got to get there at all cost!

Hear the steaming motor churning,
feel the rhythmic, rolling pulse
of the wheels convulsing, turning
as each struggles to be first,

mumbling, murmuring, making music
in a mystic monotone,
rumbling, zooming, humming magic
like a whirling gramophone

20

Got to get there, can't be last,
not a moment must be lost;
got to get there very fast,
got to get there at all cost!

See the laughing, dancing trees,
the fuzzy, hazy, dizzy trees
with shifting, rustling, romping leaves
that frolic in the flirting breeze!

Feel the wind against your faces
like a pressing rubber wall;
lean too far out of your places
and you'll have no face at all!

Got to get there, can't be last,
not a moment must be lost;
got to get there very fast,
got to get there at all cost!

What a mounting, merry madness
seeps and saps and stings your blood;
what a sizzling, shivering queerness
palpitates within your blood,

as o'er bridges steaming, streaming,
and 'round bends and curves we fly,
like a silver comet streaking
swiftly through the azure sky!

Got to get there, can't be last,
not a moment must be lost;
got to get there very fast,
got to get there at all cost!

Listen to the motor churning,
feel the rolling rhythmic pulse
of the wheels convulsing, turning
as each hurries to be first,

mumbling, murmuring, making music
in a mystic monotone,
rumbling, grumbling, humming magic
like a whirling gramophone:

> Got to get there, can't be last,
> not a moment must be lost;
> got to get there very fast,
> got to get there at all cost!

Hear the whistle echo shrilly
as the sparks begin to fly;
now the wheels behave unruly
as they squeak and screech and cry!

Who can blame them when they're never
glad as we the journeys end;
they would rather run forever
in a race that has no end!

Perhaps one of the best landmarks of our town, Sosa Hill was located at the north and the Pacific Ocean at the south of La Boca, C.Z. There were only two ways to get to La Boca by land, one was via La Boca Road from Chorillo, Republica de Panama, through Balboa, C.Z., and the other was via La Boca Road from Curundu side, circling south past the dry docks around the base of Sosa Hill, past the restaurant into La Boca. We wouldn't be adventurous in those days if as boys we didn't attempt to climb Sosa Hill, which was to us like climbing Mount Everest.

### Sosa Hill

I remember Sosa Hill,
her fervent brow warmed by the sun,
her silhouette against the sky
when dawn broke o'er the horizon,
her skirts of green, her fertile breast,
her flora and her fauna,
her winding trails, her rising crest,
her grave, mysterious, haunting look
in darkness or in pale moonlight,
her presence hovering above—
a landmark never out of sight!

Yes, I remember, once a year
her slopes became a gala sight
where fireworks went shooting up
to deck the Fourth of July night!
How we stayed up late just to see
the flares and rockets skyward bound
become bright mushrooms as they burst
in glittering colors that rained down!

And I recall her colored lights
that flashed all day and all night
upon her lofty peak to guide
uncertain ships at sea aright,
or else aircraft that sometimes came

23

too low while flying in the dark!
O what a beacon she has been
to many a lost and wandering bark!

And I remember, too, the noise
of men blasting earth on her breast;
from man's insatiable genius
she never could find peace and rest!
How they would carve at her profile
to rob her of her precious ore,
depriving and abusing her,
disfiguring her more and more!
And yet, in spite of all their doing,
today how proudly she still stands
because her destiny lies not,
nor ever will within men's hands!

Fences were built around her feet
that in my childhood were not there,
but that was when her virgin face
was brighter and seemed never sere,
when warlike strangers were not camped
between her base and lofty crest,
when a familiar, happier crowd
used to climb o'er her fervent breast!
I can remember well those times
(How fresh they still come back to me!),
and all the gay and spirited climbs
that we had made when we had played
as if we were like pirates bold
mounting with bounties from the sea
up to our rugged pirate stronghold.
Just like Captains Blackbeard and Morgan
we stood proudly atop our post
scanning the vast Pacific Ocean,
scanning the land from coast to coast!
How we stood tall in our turrets
tasting the wind against our cheeks,
and how the wind refreshed our lungs
as it blew o'er that silent peak!

We used to roam amongst her flora
courting adventure, seeking fun

as we explored along her slopes
each cave or hollow place we found!
We fantasized that we'd discover
relics and even dried old bones!
We took no chances and we armed
ourselves with little sticks and stones.
Of course there was no cause at all
for harboring any alarm—
the tiny lizards that we found
could not have done the slightest harm!

After the slopes had been explored
and, restless, we sought a new thrill,
how we rode grand toboggans near
the slippery base of Sosa Hill!
Great big palm branches were our sleds
on which we raced, and how we slid,
caring the least that we might crash
and quite frankly, often we did!

Yes, I remember so fondly,
despite the years, on Sosa Hill
were many favorite sights and scenes
that even now are haunting still.
Who can forget the picturesque scene
of the grey and white fleet coming in
with all its ships in single file
extending till vision grew dim.
From Sosa Hill you saw for miles
in all directions, north, south, east, west.
You saw the Canal installations, the docks,
the locks, the whole terrain at best—
It was a vantage point to have,
strategic military wise!
Somehow we knew that they would wave
the flag and keep us off their prize,
for we already learned too much
about warships, about their ways,
about canal security and such!
For those reasons I'm sure they raised
during the time of World War Two
the sturdy fences that were seen
when all the soldiers and the camps

invaded our stalwart queen!
But if she could have made her choice,
without a doubt one thing I know:
she would have forced all of the camps
and all the fences there to go,
and summoned back the folks who once
had climbed her and fondled her brow,
thus bringing back a sweet laughter
that sadly she does not share now!

O Sosa Hill, O Sosa Hill,
O ageless wonder that shall stand
long after we have all moved on!
O Mount Everest of my childhood,
how fondly I remember still
the climbs, the games, the sights, the fun.
Today the clearings and the trails
that we had made are long since gone!

I wrote this poem in 1972, one year after revisiting La Boca, Canal Zone, after seventeen years absence from the Isthmus, and after seeing how utterly the town was transformed. It was no longer the town we once knew. I tried to capture in these verses most of what I could remember.

**Song of La Boca**

On the shores of the Pacific
where the heartbeat is attuned
to the rhythm of the sea,
where the days are always warm
and at nights the trade winds blow,
where the air is rich and clean
and the skies above are blue,
there was once a little town
basking in the tropic sun.
In this town beside the sea,
near a high bank by the sea,
by the Panama Canal,
wood-framed tenements were built
with high sloping roofs of zinc
and with copper wire screens.
They were set on sturdy posts
standing high up from the ground;
and beneath some of these houses
there were tables, benches, chairs
like in game or parlor rooms
where the sound of dominoes
in the evenings could be heard.
Underneath some other houses
tinsmiths, tailors, carpenters
built their busy workshops, too,
and housewives hung wash and linen
in the shelter from the rain.
In this town people took pride
in their modest skills and crafts,
in their most humble apartments
which were kept spotlessly clean,
in old furniture re-polished
and shellacked to look like new,

in the suits that were from elders
proudly handed down again,
in parades and celebrations,
in worship on Sabbath days.

In this town beside the sea
where I lived, where I was born,
where we saw when I was young
the eclipsing of the sun
through pieces of broken glass
charred and blackened o'er with soot,
where we played *platillos* often
on the sidewalks and the streets,
where we played *chippon* with handballs,
played *chooflao* with stacks of beer caps
and with soda bottle caps,
where we chased the migrant butterflies
and flew homemade paper kites,
climbed tall coconut palm trees
and large spreading mango trees,
made fine flutes and whistles from
slender shoots of tall green grass,
and where after heavy rainfalls,
we played *stick-the-stick-in-the-mud,*
we knew nothing of inflation,
of stagflation or recession,
of proliferation or
of the rise and fall of stocks!
We knew nothing about taxes,
or mass violence and mass crimes!

In this town beside the sea,
near a high bank by the sea,
stood a school built wide and sturdy
overlooking the Pacific.
I can hear its brass bell ringing
from the turret on its roof;
I can see the principal
standing at the entrance door
with one hand high in the air
and a cowhide in the other
telling latecomers far off
they had better quicken stride!

I remember our pride
when our school was number one
in scholastics and in sports.
How our glee club used to sing,
*Hail to you, fair Alma Mater,*
and, on graduation day,
*Hail to you and fare-you-well!*

Down behind La Boca schoolhouse
was a beach we called *Calmetto*
with its steep and rocky shore,
with it stretch of mud and sand,
with its relics, sunken barges,
its seashells and scampering crabs!
Often when the tide was high
we would go there for a swim,
but when oil spills floated by
from the barges off the shore,
we would never venture in!
Further down Calmetto Beach,
near the east bank ferry ramp,
fishing boats were anchored there.
In the early morning hours
often when the fishermen
came back home from out to sea,
their small boats were richly laden
with a catch of tropic fish:
jacks, red snappers, bobos, brims,
fresh corbinas, mackerels.
How we looked forward to supper
and to taste a favorite dish!

Just a short walk from the school
there had stood the old clubhouse
at the southwest part of town
on the high banks near the sea.
Here we sometimes held commencements,
civic meetings, dances, plays;
and at night, its hall became
our favorite cinema
where we saw for just a dime
double-feature movie films.
Just behind the clubhouse stood

29

a most spacious tennis court
where fine tournaments were held
when the court was in its prime –
it was later cleared away
and a bakery took its place.

At the northeast part of town
where La Boca Ballpark stood,
we had played baseball like pros
with the grandstand full of fans
second-guessing, cheering wildly!
I remember regal cricket
that was played in such grand style:
players were dressed in neat white suits,
fancy caps, gloves, and shin guards.
They would swat a cricket ball,
chase it all over the field,
and would throw it in attempts
to knock down the wicket sticks.
When we had field and track meets
all the town came out to see
and to cheer their favorite stars.
At a certain time of year,
it was in the rainy season,
we would play wild soccer games.
Dressed in short pants and knee pads
and Peruvian soccer boots,
players would chase a soccer ball,
kicking it from goal to goal.
Flailing heads and feet about,
they would clash in thick mud pools
'til the uniforms they wore
looked the same and it was hard
to distinguish anyone
in those mud-packed uniforms!

There were paved streets in our town.
I recall Jamaica Prado
with its asphalt, tar-topped surface,
with its lanes going north and south
and an island in between
spread with grass, with trees and shrubs,
with bright street lights up and down,

with concrete pedestrian walks
where we strolled on Sunday evenings.
You could stand at south end and
look as far north down the Prado
till you saw La Boca Road.
Martinique Street passed the *Commy*
and the Lodge Hall 'round a curve
at the top of the embankment
facing south towards the sea,
then from there Santa Domingo
passed the clubhouse going east
past the old Salvation Army
ending at the Oil Landing Road.
Saint Thomas crossed Santa Domingo
at the south end and went north
through the very heart of town.
Barbados Street crossed the Prado,
crossed Saint Thomas going east
till it reached the baseball park.

On both sides of Barbados
eastward from Saint Thomas Street,
stood the largest tenements:
the *Titanic* and *Britannic*
each one half a block in length.
At the east side of the town
was Trinidad Street nicknamed *Gold Street*
stretching north from Santa Domingo,
past Saint Peter Baptist Church,
crossing Barbados Street
and ending at Guadeloupe,
just short of La Boca Road.
Guadeloupe Street ran parallel
to La Boca Road going west
past Saint Theresa Catholic Church
and ending at Martinique
near the commissary store.

I remember, I remember
when I was a little boy
in the early morning hours
a happy street vendor,

Haynes, came pushing his pushcart
stacked with fresh baked bread and buns
and with pastries cased in glass.
In his hand a small brass bell
tinkled far and wide and as
he came up the street, you heard
his high mellow voice singing:

*Come an' get your morning bread,*
*your morning bread,*
*get out your bed you sleepy head*
*and get your bread...*

There were other vendors, too,
like the charcoal man with pushcart
and a great big round brass gong.
We nicknamed him *Cabezon*
and for that with his gong beater
he would chase us through the town!
And there was the coconut vendor,
Mr. Gaston was his name,
but we called him *Frenchy,* too
and the old gold man who chanted,
*ol' gol'...ol' gol'... ol' gol';*

the old rag man buying rags
to be processed once again;
the raspado vendor with his
rainbow syrups in quart bottles
and the scissors grinder with his
one-wheel cart and grinding wheel
as he blew his flute in tune
calling from the yard below.

I remember Sunday mornings,
the Salvation Army band
marching on Santo Domingo
to the Salvation Army Church
near the oil landing road,
with Ms. Agard at the front
playing her triangle and tambourine
followed by the drummer and brass section.
How they played *Onward Christian Soldiers*

*Marching on to War* in unison,
not missing a single beat!

I remember Sundays were quiet
in observance of the Sabbath—
everyone was very solemn
and the churches were all packed!
In our Sunday best we worshipped
for we saved the best for church.
God-fearing and religious
no one swore or cursed on Sundays!
We refrained from most vices
except for one great sin
that I knew of—on Sunday Sabbath
most people played the lottery!
They would be glued to the radio
at eleven o'clock on Sundays
when the Panama lottery played.
It was mostly wishful thinking
for no one I knew would win!
The biggest winners always
were the government and chance vendors,
but no matter the result,
Sunday dinners were the best!
I remember in our town
Christmas was the gayest time,
what with painting, polishing,
decorating every room,
what with pies and cakes being baked,
with singing of Christmas songs,
with the games, the gifts and fun!
There's a scene I still recall:
Mr. Armstrong's two-piece band
entertaining in the streets!
A flutist and drummer played
in fast time while Armstrong danced
in costume the *gully root*
as they went from block to block.
But the most uproarious scene
Was *'fuera Con el viejo* or
*Old Year's Night* as it was called.
Crowds of boys who stayed awake
went marching through town at midnight

33

beating old pans, buckets, drums
singing out in unison:

> *'Fuera con el viejo,*
> *pum-pum-pum,*
> *'Fuera con el viejo,*
> *pum-pum-pum!*

There are old familiar scenes
that I still recall today,
like the icehouse in the morning
with long lines of people waiting
with their carts and crocus bags
to buy blocks sold by the pound
for their iceboxes at home;
like the bustling commissary
on a busy Saturday morning:
crowds of shoppers loaded down
or else waiting to be served.
In those days we had no credit,
Master Charge nor VISA cards,
only green and blue coupon books
issued out of wages earned.
There were no store fronts in town,
neon signs or noisy bars,
no nightclubs, or *greasy spoons*.
There was just one restaurant
that closed up at nine o'clock.
We had a wood-framed Chinese shop
on the northern edge of town
just across La Boca Road.
There we'd go often to buy
*kwatti* this and *kwatti* that:
rice, brown sugar, fresh lettuce,
*micha* bread, butter and oils,
penny's worth of cigarettes.
It was wild to see how much
just one buffalo head could buy!

I recall the ferry road
at the northwest edge of town
that led to the ferry ramp.
Back and forth along this road

all the cars and trucks went by.
They would pile onto the ferry
that went to and from each shore
of the Panama Canal.
Coming from the western shore,
trucks were loaded with livestock:
smelly cows, pigs and chickens,
and fruits from interior farms
on their way to market stalls,
*sal-si-puedes,* butcher shops,
and to many grocery stores
in the heart of Panama.

Not far from the ferry road
I recall a dead-end street
that was lined with bamboo trees.
Where it ended were footpaths
that led to the waterfront
and docks where we used to go
to see giant battle ships
and free movies on their screens.
The Main Street, or LA Boca Road
passed by the restaurant
and then circled out of town
by a rock crusher where all day
rocks were crushed and piled up high.
I remember many walks
on this circling road that went
'round the base of Sosa Hill
till it passed a certain place
where banana stalls and stands
at the roadside were being manned
by old native men and women
selling wares mostly to tourists
off the ships docked in the pier.
Somewhere on this circling road
just before you reached the stalls
was a gateway to the docks.
Often when I was a boy
I had entered that gateway
as I took with me my father's
lunch bag slung over my arm.
I walked by the old dry docks,

marveled at the great big pit
lined with massive concrete walls.
Sometimes it was quite a while
that I stood there at this pit
till a ship was towed inside,
when a great concrete floodgate
that had opened closed again
and the water was drained out
of the chamber with the ship,
and a dripping ship was left
upon giant props to dry.
Then masked welders would go down,
torches blaze and rivets fly,
while cranes raised and lowered down
parts they used to fix her hull.
Across this pit that was so deep
it made you dizzy looking down,
a bridge stretched out to you.
It was narrow with few rails.
I would cross this narrow bridge
and continue on the way
to my father where he worked.
He worked far beyond the dry docks
near a point where ships would pass
on their way through the canal.
He would go out in a boat
to set oil lamps onto poles
that would signal there was danger
and guide ships away from shore.

I remember in La Boca,
anywhere you chose to stand,
if you looked towards the north
you could see the lofty peak
and the lights of Sosa Hill.
Her array of flashing lights
I supposed signaled to ships
or to aircraft flying by.
I recall in early days,
Fourth of July fireworks
were set off on Sosa Hill.
They lit up the skies with mushrooms
that exploded in designs,

glittering colors that rained down
each burst brighter than the last!

Now it seems like yesterday
that my father farmed the land
on a farm on *Far Fan* Hill
beyond the Pan Canal West Bank
overlooking the Canal.
Often we went there together
and we tilled and worked the land:
all morning we cleared and planted
and at noon would rest awhile.
How I loved to scan the horizon,
name the ships in harbor and
count the ones sailing away
with courses set for adventure
somewhere far across the sea!

Looking northward, we could see
our modest little town—
we could see off in the distance
the clubhouse, playground, school,
every zinc-patched sloping rooftop,
and the moving specks of people.
In the background, Sosa Hill,
always staring back at you,
beamed her flashing, colored lights
as if winking in delight!
It was hard to turn away
from this view on Far Fan Hill
and return to farming chores.
When at last the harvest came,
we brought home abundant crops
which we shared with friends and neighbors.

It was not so long ago
I returned across the sea
to this land that nurtured me.
I returned longing to see
at the least some sights I knew;
but although I stood again
and walked on my native soil,
I saw no familiar places!

They had vanished like a dream!
They were gone the streets I knew,
all the sloping rooftop houses,
the clubhouse, school, restaurant,
Chinese garden, ferry, too,
and the people who lived there!
Not a vestige anywhere
save a piece of concrete slab
where the restaurant once stood!
'Twas as if a painter came
with a paintbrush in his hand,
wiped an old painting away,
then upon the same canvas
painted there a different place,
painted there a different story
that I could not even trace!
It's a feeling not for words
when you leave and then return
to the place where you were born,
but the town's no longer there
and the people have all gone!

The only link now to the past
lies in memories that you keep,
that bring pangs into your breast
and a swelling to your eyes!
Yet there's one witness who stands
there today, her lips though sealed:
Sosa Hill will always be
a landmark in history!
If her lips could only speak
she could tell the world so much
of the goings and the comings,
of the drama that was there,
of the people and their lives,
of the birth, the growth and death
of a humble little town
that once flourished at her feet
on the shores of the Pacific
by the Panama Canal.

Long ago when La Boca, Canal Zone was still young, early every morning a street vendor named Haynes would push a four-wheel glass-enclosed cart all the way from Panama City into La Boca Town to sell his freshly baked bread and pastries.  It was a good business for him while it lasted since his entire cartload of liberty bread, French biscuit, sweet breads, *roli poli's,* etc. was sold out before he got onto La Boca road to head back into Panama. Later, Mr. Haynes was put out of business—at least his La Boca route was—when the canal zone government outlawed street vendors from coming into the canal zone to sell their wares. They said it was for health reasons or it was illegal, or something to that effect, and refused to allow any vendors on the canal zone; but that's another story. In any case, this poem is my childhood recollection of our beloved pastry vendor named Haynes.

**The Pastry Vendor**

At half past five before the sun
came shining through in splendor,
afar off you could hear the sound
of Haynes, the pastry vendor.

At first his small brass bell rang out,
tintinnabulating,
and then his tenor voice sang out
his favorite vendor's calling:

*Come and get your morning bread,*
*your morning bread,*
*get out your bed, you sleepy head,*
*and get your bread!*

Awake and dashing out the door,
I headed straight towards the street
to join that happy troubadour
as helper on his morning beat!

We pushed the cart and rang the bell,
tasks that we did, but not for pay;
instead we got a special treat
of luscious pastry everyday.

A hot sweet bun, turnover or
fresh *yucca pone* or biscuit,
or piece of coconut pie was more
than worth the effort for it!

Each day at half past five he came
for years and without failure,
until one day was not the same
without our pastry vendor.

We knew not why he did not come
again and soon stopped asking;
but how we missed his happy song
at half past five in the morning!

When I was about five or six years old, I
could hardly wait to hear the eight musical notes
played by the scissors grinder on his flute whenever
he passed through the streets of La Boca. He
pedaled a funny-looking contraption that looked like
a tricycle with a huge grindstone wheel in the back.
I so liked the sound of his flute that I wanted to get
one for Christmas. When she heard his flute, my
mother would call out to the next-door neighbor,
"The scissors grinder is here!...The scissors
grinder...!" and I would run downstairs behind her
so I wouldn't miss the show for anything!
Housewives would gather around him, and each in
turn would have her scissors or knives sharpened. I
tried to capture the experience in my poem.

**The Scissors Grinder**

Every time the scissors grinder
came to town, my mom, you'd find her
ready with dull knives and scissors!
That he was not far away
no one even had to tell her,
she could hear his high-pitched flute play
eight tones ever bright and clear,
the sweetest music to my ear:
do mi sol mi, do mi sol do,
*Scissors to grind!*
*Sharpen so fine!*

Suddenly he would be standing
in the yard with people there,
with his right foot busy pumping,
hands guiding the blades with care,
with the grindstone swiftly spinning
as he pressed the blades so near;
then the grinding wheel went humming
as the cold steel touched it bare,
and the metals seemed to cry
as their sparks began to fly!

How I loved to watch him pedal

(such a strange-looking contraption!),
as the crankshaft turned the spindle
around which the grindstone spun
biting steel of knives and scissors.
He would test his craftsmanship
on the open edge of scissors,
touching it with fingertip,
      and if pleased, he nodded to you
      indicating he was through!

When the last scissor was sharpened,
then his strange-looking contraption
was a cart-on-wheel he shortened,
and he soon pedaled along.
As he traveled far away
you could hear his eight-tone flute play,
do mi sol mi, do mi sol do,
*I'm on my way, I'm on my way*
and then his roundelay:
      *Scissors to grind!*
      *Sharpen so fine!*

Mr. Gaston was a Frenchman from Martinique who used to set up his pushcart on Martinique Street near its intersection with Barbados Street, where there were lots of passers-by. My parents knew him well, and I often helped him. In return, I could drink all the coconut water and eat all the coconut I wanted. One day a passerby bantered with him:

### The Coconut Vendor

Mister Gaston, Mister Gaston!
what a bunch of coconuts!
How you sell them, Mister Gaston,
can I get one for a *nyap*?

*Cooocanat!!..cooocanat!!*
*Don' mek joke, two for a dime!*
*Cooocanat!!..cooocanat!!..*
*My machete slice it one time!*

Mister Gaston, Mister Gaston!
what a bunch of coconuts!
'ere's two bits now! Give me this one,
make it this one, that an' that!

*Cooocanat!!.. watah cooocanat!!*
*Young or old, 'ces son bon manger oui'!*
*Cooocanat!!.. watah cooocanat!!*
*Jelly rich, milk so sweet mes amis!*

Mister Gaston, Mister Gaston,
with your thick *moostash* an' hat!
Swing your machete, Mister Gaston,
slice that *joocy cocanat!*

*Cooocanat!!.. watah cooocanat!!*
*Tek some home for yuh dear chou chou!*
*Cooocanat!!.. watah cooocanat!*
*mek nice drink après diner, too!*

Mister Gaston, Mister Gaston,
with your strange accent at that!
Mister Gaston, where you come from?
Slice that *joocy cocanat!*

*Me a come from Martinique;*
*me a Frenchi, yuh know dat,*
*can't yuh tell it when I speak?*
*No more talk, buy cocanat!*

Mister Gaston, Mister Gaston,
by the streetside with pushca't,
now your long day's work is done
'cause there's no more *cocanat!*

*Cooocanat!!..no more cooocanat!!*
*tomorrow Frenchy come again!*
*Cooocanat!!..watah cooocanat,*
*come a sunshine, or come a rain!*

A few enterprising women in our town would do hairdressing, some would take in sewing, and some would also make and sell food items such as homemade ice cream, *duro* (fruit-flavored ice cubes), pastries, etc. One of these enterprising women, Mrs. Messiah, set up a cook shop and food business right under her house and did a thriving business. This poem is about her. I loved to eat her *chip chip* (sugared coconut brittle)!

**The *Chip Chip* Lady**

*Under the house* she stood,
an apron 'round her waist,
selling such tasty food
that never went to waste!

Around about evening time,
especially on pay day,
in her somewhat sweet rhyme
this is what she would say:

*Come, buy, come buy chip chip,*
*for all who got sweet lip;*
*come buy hot black puddin'*
*eat it an' know good livin;*

*come, come don' shy wit money,*
*an' buy some sousse too, honey,*
*mek chests grow big and hairy,*
*listen to the chip chip lady!*

*Under the house* she stood,
an apron 'round her waist,
selling all sorts of food
that never went to waste.

On weekends I was there
and this is not a boast,
people from everywhere
said her cooking was the most!

45

*Come buy fresh hot meat patti,*
*will make yuh stomach happy;*
*buy yucca pone, too, deari,*
*wash i' dung wi' gingabeer!*

*Come, try fry fish now, honey,*
*Or fishcake warm and ready;*
*An' tell yuh friends, too, deari,*
*Come an' see the chip chip lady!*

*Under the house* she stood,
an apron 'round her waist,
and the food would taste so good
that nothing went to waste.

All the youths and adults, too,
loved to come and buy her food;
there was no one else I knew
who could make *chip chip* so good!

Somehow a silly rumor went around that Mr. Cumberbatch, the policeman, was the naked man who was terrorizing women after dark in La Boca Town. Well, when Ms. Doubtful heard the rumor from Ms. Sing Song she took exception to it. This is an excerpt from their conversation in West Indian lingo.

### A Fe Wen Yuh La La a Good Man's Name

*Sarah, Sarah,* said Mary Sing Song,
*me yeari seh de naked man
wa fe frighten all de ladies dem
is Cumberbatch the policeman!*

Those words sent a sudden chill
through the nerves of Sarah doubtful,
and in her consternation
she let out quite a mouthful:

*A fe wha, a fe wha yuh da seh?
de naked man? Wha Lawd, noh!
no weh, no weh, no weh,
not de Cumberbatch me a know!*

*Chile de Cumberbatch me a know
'im a fine policeman me sweari;
Lawd 'im could shoot yuh know;
Dem cawl 'im de Bull yuh yeari!*

*When yuh see 'im cum dung de street
eena 'im kahky unifo'm,
bad bwoize a trebul a de feet;
befoh 'im cum dem a gone!*

*An' 'im no 'fraid fe man nor fe beece!
Me de feel La Boca Tung
was safah 'cause 'im kep de peece;
'pon dat me wudda kis de grung!*

*Cumberbatch! Chile, a fe yuh go weh,*
*'im no naked man, lawd, noh!*
*me kyan believe it no weh,*
*not de Cumberbatch me a know!*

Then Ms. Sing Song declared that she, too,
had her doubts but at any rate,
*Is hard to know these days w'at's true,*
*but I gwine investigate!*

*Yes, yes, yuh bettah do dat chile*
*'cause befoh yuh go broadcast it,*
*when yuh la la a good man's name*
*mek dyam sure the story fit!*

The plantain was almost like a staple food; it was quite plentiful and was grown in the gardens and local farms that many West Indian workers cultivated. When ripe, it was very sweet and was eaten fried or raw. The Latinos called the fried sweet plantain *maduros*. The green plantain, however, just like the green banana, was cooked and often prepared like mashed potato or yam. It was served by itself or as a supplement to rice, potato and yam in many dishes. It is the subject of this poem and the cause of a nickname being given to the worker in the poem.

**Pound Plantain**

Blackburn, you know, was a hard man to please!
His *missus* found out one thing he liked
was plantain pound with some *gunga* peas;
so all she did like any good wife
was give him pound plantain every day of his life.

Well now, he went 'long with that for some time,
but one day when things didn't go so well
he came home with a hurt inside, so he was primed
when he sat down for supper and his eyes fell
'pon the table with pound plantain piled high as hell!

Blackburn got so mad he took up the plate
and went outside to show the next door neighbor.
*look wha' my mary give to me, I'm so irate;*
*'s a dyam shame after all o' my hard labor*
*I comes home to eat an' I can't get nothin' better!*

*I brings home my two-fifty book, pung plantain!*
*I brings home my five-dollar book, pung plantain!*
*I brings home my seven-fifty book, pung plantain!*
*Ev'ry Christ day all I gets is pung plantain!*
*Man, I ain' goin' take no more o' this pung plantain!*

And before the rage left his head, straightway
Blackburn threw the food in the garbage can,
but what he didn't know was that from that day
story went about town and a rhyme began,
which all the children learned by heart and sang:

*Ev'ry day, pung plantin!*
*Monday, Tuesday, pung plantin!*
*Wednesday, Thursday, pung plantin!*
*Two-fifty book, pung plantin!*
*Five-dollar book, pung plantin!*

And as the story goes, he got that nickname
any time he passed by going down the street.
Both he and his two boys in the same vein
were called, *Pung Plantin an' de Pungeez*, to wit,
for the plantain diet they used to eat.

In La Boca we had our own variations of Caribbean accents, like the Bajan or Martiniquan, or Jamaican, but in general we all sounded alike more or less. To this day my Caribbean accent sometimes slips out, especially when I get angry! When I first arrived in New York from La Boca, C.Z., people here knew right away that I had a Caribbean background from my speech; most of the time, though, I didn't think you could tell very much.

Back in the days, when Americans came to our community, their accents also stood out markedly to us. Like Mr. Neely, an American who was once appointed by the U.S. government as the Secretary of the La Boca Clubhouse. In a very twangy or nasal voice he would say, "Yuh could be Tudah kid or could be Tudah goat, mane, mane, git ta hell out a hyar." We thought Americans sounded funny, just as they must have thought we sounded. Well now, about this poem. Lennon was a native Caribbean son born and raised in La Boca and sounded like a Caribbean all his life, until one day, and his mom didn't take too kindly to it either. Here is the poem:

**Solomon Bolosky Lennon**

They nicknamed him *Bolosky*
after an African
by the name of Solomon Bolosky,
an Abyssinian,
that's what I have been told!

His real surname was Lennon.
I don't recall his first,
so I'll just call him Solomon
or Sol, whichever fits the verse,
to let the tale unfold!

When Solomon worked in Gorgas,
as orderly no less,
one day a certain patient was
leaving for the U.S. and impressed
with *Sol Bolosky Lennon,*

offered to take dear Sol as well
as his private orderly,
which seemed quite fine, as one could tell,
for Sol had never been to sea—
but he was changed from then on!

He packed his bags and luggage
and left town in fine style;
you'd think with extra baggage
he would be gone a long, long while;
that's what his friends inferred!

The truth is, when he reached New York
his so-so benefactor
got off alone at New York port
and left Sol in the harbor,
on board ship heading homeward!

Before he left town Sol didn't say,
for all his boastful ardor,
that his stay in the U.S.A.
would be in New York harbor
on board the ship that brought him!

So with this background, it was strange
when he returned one day
and there was such a startling change
in him, no one knew what to say
and thought it was a whim!

For Solomon went off a *Bajee;*
he sailed across the sea
and came back home a damn *Yankee*
a-yanking fluently,
but that's not where it ends.

When he came *Yankeefying*
he called out to his maw: *Saay, Maaam,*
*send a boy down hyar to git mah thengs!*
She yelled, *Bring dem yuh dyam self, yuh*
*dyam foo foo, a yuh yankee?...since whens?*

People were given nicknames for various reasons. Sometimes it was because of a physical characteristic, or an amusing remark attributed to them, or the way they walked or talked, or what they ate, or because of an incident or event that happened to them. Many times I didn't even know or remember their Christian names, only their pseudonyms. In many cases the nicknames stuck and in some cases they didn't, depending on the individuals. A few examples of these creative nicknames that I can remember are: *Pung Plantin, Bakes and Liver, Blow Blow, Thin Lizzy, Baby Boy, Blackout, Twist Up, Feet, Putty Knife, The Bull, Big Tree, Beppo, Rippo, Rancho, Lucho, Bongo, Boozo, Bumbilo, Bawli, Boisi, Dapper, Peacock, Sampung, Snoogy, Keppie, Playboy, Yacca, and Blackshirt.* So it was not surprising how the nickname in this poem came about.

### Dog Bite Me, Cat Scratch Me

In the course of events in our little town
a good piece of gossip never failed to amuse,
and word could so quickly get around
that the moment something happened, it was news!

Take for instance when a certain person well known
came home one night after playing around!
He made the mistake of not coming straight home
and spent some time with his sweetie in town!

Well, when this playboy came home that night
late for supper and with a look of guilt,
his wife was suspicious but she kept very quiet
for a minute before letting him know how she felt.

Then she raised a big ruckus for his coming home late,
and cussed him and needled him in every way
hoping to make him so irate
that in anger he would accidentally say

what it was he did or what was done to make him
act like a rat who had swallowed a cat
and who had no intention of ever revealing
his secret! She could forget about that!

So he weathered the storm and got it in his head
that the worst was over; but the missus refused
to quit, and when he undressed to prepare for bed,
she checked every piece down to his socks for clues!

Meanwhile, playboy took a bath; it was a good idea,
but soap and water couldn't wash the stains out!
As he left the shower, she eyed him straightway,
and he finally had the gumption to open his mouth,

*Woman, why you bother me so! Leave me alone, you hear!*
And before he could turn away, she looked at him again,
His chest and back bore teeth marks and scratches everywhere,
*Lawd, Lawd,* she cried, *now how you goin' explain*

*those teeth marks and scratches that wasn't there before?*
*You bettah talk up quick and make it good this time*
*before I kill you and send you back to your gutter whore,*
*you good-for-nothing dog you, you piece o' slime!*

And as she was about to strike him with a hot iron,
he hollered, *Dog bite me, cat scratch me, let me explain!*
*Dog bite you, cat scratch you, well now is a angry she lion*
*goin' bludgeon you brain and teach you not to cheat on me*
*again!*

Playboy grabbed his clothes and ran out of the house
'cause he knew he was guilty of cheating on his wife!
And for days he had to sleep *under the cellar,* like a louse,
and he never cheated on her again for the rest of his life!

When that incident happened, right away word got around,
the very same night, in fact, and from that day on
one *playboy* became famous in the tales of our town
and was called *Dog Bite Me, Cat Scratch Me* in rhyme and
song!

It did not happen too often, but occasionally some neighbors did have a squabble between them. It was never a pretty sight even If they later made up when their blood cooled down, and they felt the shame, embarrassment and resentment of the rest of the town. I knew of one such incident that caused me to write this poem.

## The Quarrel

Two neighbors quarreled all day long
until their voices coarse and strong
reverberated through the town
and summoned all the ears around.

A querying throng then gathered 'round
the warriors who strove to astound
with shocking deeds and fiery tongue
all those who looked and listened on.

One neighbor, like a stolid ape,
revealed a most distorted shape
to mock the other who now scoffed
and in like fashion started off

a pantomime; the audience laughed
and laughed to witness such witchcraft!
Then words began to fly from each,
the next a lesson aimed to teach;

but what rare blend of expletives
in volumes of high explosives!
Each cursed the hat the other bore,
each cursed the shoes the other wore,

right down the whole ancestral tree
of each, each shouted blasphemy,
which made the audience writhe and roar
and, well amused, cry out for more!

The devil in his blazing hole
could not his wild laughter control!
And so all night they carried on
until it was the following dawn,

then with a final vulgar show
they ended all further ado,
but only from exhaustion, though,
thank Heaven they at last did so!

The crowd dispersed its weary forms,
then came the calm that follows storms,
and you, a stranger, would not dream
that here had been a shocking scene!

The town again quite easily
returned to light activity,
while two hearts—thinking each had won
a victory from the other one,

thinking that each had rightly done
a duty to correct a wrong,
and the adversary alone
had paid dearly for stepping on

each other's pride—were wrong for each,
too vain, had only served to teach
how bleak was each one's unchaste soul,
for that was all the quarrel told!

If I did not see for myself and know of this couple, I would not have believed that two people could literally be so close and inseparable in everything they did. They both seemed to relish the bond between them, and they told the rest of the world to mind their own business; that that was the way they chose to live their lives. In a way, I admired them very much!

### June and July

Two *Bajans* called June and July
lived in on our town in forty-two.
They had no *picknee* that's no lie,
they stuck together just like glue,
'cause every time when June went by,
you looked close by, there was July.

July, I heard tell, was that way
'cause she was married twice, you know.
Some husband snatcher came one day
and stole her first spouse—what a blow!
Since then she swore she'd make damn sure
she didn't lose this one like the one before!

And that is why when June went by
(woe on all snatchers with designs!)
watchful July was very close by
to stop them and to change their minds.
*June and July!* we called to them,
and they would cuss us now and then.

When you saw June walk down the street,
right 'pon his heels July kept pace;
she cared nothing about being discreet—
guarding her man was no disgrace!
Neither one of them was in sight
without the other one day and night!

June would go out, July went too;
June went downstairs, July went too;
June crossed the street, July crossed too;
July went to market, sure 'nough June, too;
June took out the garbage can,
July went 'long to give a hand!

So in the realm of relationships,
if you have witnessed togetherness,
or thought you had seen companionships,
you still haven't seen anything yet,
believe me, unless with your own eye
you've seen the likes of June and July!

This was a race that signified a strong personal rivalry between two men who did not like each other very much. Their personalities were quite opposite, as one was fiery and flamboyant, and the other was very cautious and reserved. It was a race of two different styles and temperaments—not that that had anything to do with the outcome, but the readers can judge for themselves.

### The Bicycle Race

The die was cast, the stage was set
for Messrs. Murphy and Bynoe.
Who was the faster cyclist yet,
the whole town was waiting to know
before the famous showdown.

Just who were these leviathans,
eager to prove their cycling powers
before a crowd of anxious fans
in one of rivalry's best hours
in old La Boca Town?

*Bynoe the fox*, folks used to say,
like the time he nearly lost his head
when he was walking home one day
and he beheld a prize outspread
just waiting for him in the grass!

As he reached down to grab the purse
another swifter hand was there;
then Bynoe cried, *Oi seen it first,
is half and half; oi wants moi share!*
and walked into a trap, alas!

His would-be mugger said, slyly,
*les go behind yonder great stone
an' I'll give yuh yours, don' wurry!*
Then Bynoe sensed a funny tone
and saw a look of treachery!

That's when he high-tailed out of there,
escaping foul play in that place,
or else this tale would end right here
and the Bynoe-Murphy classic race
would not go down in history!

Back to the race! Each day Bynoe
practiced and practiced on the sly!
Without a word, off he would go
atop his cycle, whizzing by
around and around La Boca track.

Murphy would laugh when they told him
Bynoe was training for the meet.
*Look-a-yere now, oi don' need no trainin';*
*oi'll wip 'ee gud ev'n in moi sleep,*
Murph said, turning slightly his back,

and then added, *An' woh is more*
*oi gets awl de trainin' oi needs;*
*ev'ry Chrois day ten moils ohr more*
*oi pumps to work fast loik a steed...*
*an' oi ain' never toir'd yet!*

*Boino need de trainin', le' 'ee go 'long;*
*oi' will lap 'ee ten toims, yuh goin' see!*
*oi is Murfee yuh 'noh, oi is strong,*
*an' woh is more, oi'l be happee*
*to lai a pung peece; yuh goin' bet?*

Well, Murphy's mouth wasn't all he had;
you see, Murph loved a lot of *juice*.
They used to steal the stuff so bad
the warehouse tried to stem the abuse
and switched to denatured alcohol!

They did not know who was the culprit,
but warned about the poison so
no one dared steal... 'cept Murphy with
his strong passion for juice! Oh no,
he couldn't lay off the juice at all!

So when one day the work crew saw
Murphy drinking the alcohol,
they just stood there gaping in awe—
*How 'ee don' die?* was what they all
wondered! But here's Murphy's reply:

*Oi ain' no fool, see oi ain' ded,*
*cawz oi is smahta dan awl woono!*
*Yuh see dis ere moldie, rancid bred,*
*oi strains awl de pois'n out loik soh—*
*it even taste bettah, woono troi!*

And that was how Murphy revealed
his unusual resourcefulness.
With all his mouth he was quite skilled,
ev'n if booze was one mistress
he couldn't resist, nor cared to try.

At last the big day had arrived—
a sunny Saturday afternoon!
The stands and ballpark came alive;
along the track there was no room
as at the starting post they stood!

These two who waged a bitter feud
and months of angry words as foes
stood in a tense, unfriendly mood—
good thing it was not fists they chose
with which to settle their grudge feud!

Murphy started to psyche Bynoe,
*Boino, yuh goin' lose, woi yuh don' witdraw;*
*a goin' mek yuh eat John Crow!*
*oi's de bes' ting on wheels, moi craw*
*achin' to wip yuh tail!*

Bynoe remained serious and silent.
Not even a glance he gave Murphy,
but bridled on his bike, intent
to catch the starter's signal; he
just had to beat this *moutah massee!*

The starter raised his pistol high,
*On your mark! get set!* Bang! Off they broke!
Murphy shot out—how he could fly!
The race looked like it was a joke
the way it started, all Murphy!

But Bynoe was no fool; you see,
his plan was, 'let Murphy burn out
while he paced himself purposely,
saving his strength, without a doubt,
for the homestretch quarter mile.'

Murphy was way out front, ten lengths,
waving out to the crowd, clowning,
gloating with overconfidence!
Slowly, Bynoe started gaining,
which was his game plan and his style!

It seemed that Bynoe's plan made sense;
about halfway the lead reduced
to five lengths; three quarters, three lengths;
and for the first time Murph deduced
that he was in a serious race!

He pumped but all he pumped, Bynoe
was on his tail, closing the gap,
and Murphy worried, *Blas' yuh, Boino,*
*yuh ain' goin' pass me, one moh lap*
*to go, an' oi's de winnah of dis race!*

But Murphy wasn't as strong as when
he started; that brought him no joy!
Bynoe thought, *Oi'l let 'ee tail win'*
*wuk fuh me so oi'l pass ee boi*
*insoid de homestretch, ef'n oi don' fall!*

And what seemed like a joke at first
became a classic race on turf,
fans yelled until their throats nearly burst,
*C'mon Boino, C'mon Murph!*
as two old rivals gave it all!

Three hundred yards before the tape
Bynoe called on his last reserve;
thank Heaven he was in good shape,
he passed Murphy on the last curve
then pulled away just as he planned!

And Bynoe crossed the finish line
two lengths in front of Murphy who
swore it was *obyah* of some kind
that Bynoe used because he knew
he, Murphy, was the better man.

But all who saw that famous race
knew better, and the record stood:
Bynoe had run a smarter race
and beat *moutah massey* Murphy good
on the old La Boca ballground!

There never was another race
or rivalry quite like that one,
which brought a thrill time can't erase
though Murphy and Bynoe are gone,
as well as old La Boca Town!

I guess I was too young at the time when the great horserace took place in Juan Franco race track in Panama City. I relate it only from stories I heard from old timers when I was a boy. You could say it was a lot of hype and a case of great expectations that failed to materialize and that led to great disappointment, embarrassment, and injured pride for a lot of people. It was one of those stories that was happily allowed to fade away into time and forgetfulness.

## Jonathan G

From waaaay back, Bajans' pride was something!
They couldn't stand all the local bragging
About the fastest hoss alive!
There was too much loud talk, fuss and jive

'bout de 'rabian hoss, or the hoss from dis place
or de hoss from that place—such a disgrace!
You'd think dem's de only ones had a hoss!
Man, it mek the Bajans become so cross

till they, too, soon started to brag,
'boas'ing' that they had the fastest nag;
that's when they brought the great Jonathan G
way 'cross the sea from Bajan country!

An' a big something was made of it
all over town, in the homes and the street,
till it beat by far all phenomena
when Jonathan G came to Panama.

So many was counting on that hoss
and they boasted till the boasting was gross;
how they brag, brag, brag, brag, brag, brag, brag
'bout that famous Bajan nag!

soon the race was set, it was Jonathan
against the hosses of the land;
but before the showdown race began,
there wasn't one single Barbadian

who didn't put down a little piece
on Jonathan, or at the least
wave a banner or some kind of flag
for their most prestigious nag.

Well now, the hippodrome was jam packed
and the colors and the banners were all stacked,
and the bets of all amounts were in,
the biggest one, Jonathan G to win!!

As the thoroughbreds stood at the starting gate,
eyes were fixed, hearts in a nervous state,
then the gates opened and away they went
in a thunderous cloud as if hell bent!!

But for some reason, halfway 'round the track
Jonathan G seemed to be *laying back*!
How could that be? It must be a trick
or else he was planning a last-minute kick!

Everybody knew that strategy,
to come from behind; it look pretty
to see a hoss bolt out from last to first;
so they waited for that last minute burst!

But, sad to say, it didn't go that way
When the finish line was crossed that day!
Poor Jonathan G was less than fast;
in point of fact he came dead last!

How pride fell, Lawd! But even more,
a lot of savings was lost for sure!
And whenever the name of Jonathan G
is mentioned today, folks act strangely.

Now that's the story as told to me
about the famous Jonathan G,
the racehorse from Barbados land,
the fastest hoss from here to Siam!

When I was a boy in La Boca Town, I used to see some elderly West Indian men always with a stick in their hand. I used to think they carried it to balance themselves and to keep from falling, or that it was some kind of status symbol like an African elder's stick. I came to find out one day that the stick was more than just a walking stick; in fact, it was a formidable weapon and as lethal as a prizefighter's fists or a spear or a gun, in the hands of a skilled *stickman*. Mr. Harper was such a man. This poem is about him.

**West Indian Stickman**

Let me tell you 'bout a great stickman
in the days when I was young;
his name was Mr. Harper, and
he lived in La Boca Town!

You would think because he had a limp
that he could not fight a lick;
but don't give an old West Indian
the short end of the stick!

You can ask one *Putty Knife* who knows
'cause he felt Mr. Harper's hand;
let me tell you how they came to blows,
one bully versus one stickman.

Putty Knife was mean with his two fists
and he punched poor Leon one;
Leon was no match for Putty's fists
but he was Mr. Harper's son.

Leon cried, went home and told his pa
what that Putty Knife had done;
Harper grabbed Leon and his *stick-o'-war*
and headed for the showdown.

When they reached the clubhouse poolroom,
there was Putty still playing pool;
in the room, a hush fell everywhere
and Putty Knife was cool!

67

He saw when the old man walked in
but pretended he didn't see;
with cue stick in hand, and a mean grin
he was ready as can be.

Harper made the first move when he said,
*You there, you the one hit my boy?*
Putty Knife didn't say a word; instead
he just held the cue like a toy!

*I'm talking to you,* Harper said again.
*You the one what hit my boy?*
Putty still ignored, turning his back then
towards Harper like some ploy.

Harper wouldn't take this insult though,
and nudged Putty in the back;
by the time he did, Putty swung his cue
and there was a very loud *crack*!

You see, Harper timed just right the swing
and whipped out his stick like that!
In a flash you saw sticks parrying
back and forth with frightful impact!

Putty swung; the old man parried the blow
and countered to the midriff;
Putty buckled with a grin somehow,
but that grin was no relief.

He swung back, the old man ducked, and before
Putty Knife could settle down,
the old man jabbed his ribs once more
and struck him on his crown.

Putty got real mad and serious then
and swung the cue like a madman;
his wildness only hastened his end
at the hands of a great stickman.

Harper blocked each blow, hit him in the stomach
and caught him on the shinbone;
Putty Knife buckled; he got a whack
on his back and gave a weird groan.

He was dangerous still, the old man knew,
so he had to finish him off now;
he sidestepped a desperate lunging cue
and returned a telling blow

right across the head, *whack*, and that was all!
Putty went down slow, the fight was o'er,
messing with a stickman was his downfall...
he would mess with him no more!

This is a sad story about the only murder-suicide that I recall ever happening in our town. The names of the participants are not important, but everybody in the town in those days knew about it. It was just a sad case of two young people who got caught up in the game of betrayal and philandering that went wrong!

### The *Shippy* and the Housewife

The stars, faded on this dark night,
in somber vigilance look down;
with mournful sounds, the winds unite
and send a chill throughout the town.

On such a night, fate chose a spot
beneath the pale face of the moon
to spin a tale too soon forgot
of two hearts hastened to their doom!

He was a *shippy* off a ship
enjoying leave from sea duty;
she was a housewife; a slight limp
did not detract from her beauty.

He was the quiet, serious kind;
she was a restless, pampered wife.
He had a mating on his mind;
she craved the finer things of life.

They first met at a friend's one night,
the seaman and the roving wife;
his fires of love were burning bright;
she had a hungry zest for life!

And as the wheels of fortune turned
with two who never should have met,
they launched their romance unconcerned
that it might be their ruin yet.

He brought her rubies, silks and pearls,
and gifts from far across the sea.
Her eyes lit up to see such pearls.
he said, *Some day you'll marry me!*

She sneaked away to be with him
at first, but later did not care
and lived a double life in sin,
flaunting her lover everywhere!

And she would laugh, and she would sing;
she thought it all was just a game!
Why could she not have everything—
take what she pleased or leave the same?

But when her lover came to her,
quite candidly to her he'd say,
*Divorce your husband! The sooner
you're free, we'll be married that day!*

She said, *That would take time to do
and plenty money with which to sue!*
He went to sea and came anew,
and brought with him a fortune, too!

She took it all, he left again;
she thought that she was very wise
and spent it on fine clothes and gems,
and gave away fine gifts likewise.

And when the *shippy* came again,
she told him she would soon be free:
*You must be patient*, she told him,
*if you intend to marry me!*

So this went on until one day
her lover could take it no more;
he stopped her when she tried to say
the same line that she said before,

*Next time I come, be ready then,*
he said, *for I will marry you;*
*and here's some more money to spend,*
*this time be sure to make it do!*

When he returned, the skies were dark,
the stars were faint, the pale moon shone;
the mournful winds howled through the park,
and sent a chill throughout the town!

The lovers met—she brought a friend—
her eyes were glazed and somewhat grim;
she told him that it was the end,
that she could never marry him!

She waited then for his response,
and saw him reach into his bosom;
her instincts made her leap at once
for he had pulled a lethal gun!

He said, *No need to try to run!*
He pointed and he shot her dead!
And then he turned the lethal gun
and shot himself right through the head!

Sometimes on dark and dismal nights
when stars look pale, and all about
the winds are howling loud, you might
still hear those screams and shots ring out!

In the early days of La Boca, in my childhood I recall, mango trees and various tropical trees were planted on every block and a horse-driven water wagon (which we called Hokus Pokus) used to come around daily to water the trees and shrubs until they were grown. Also, to illuminate the town at night, tall street lamps with brilliant light bulbs enclosed in glass domes were erected on many street corners. Here the youth often gathered to banter and to polemicize before retiring for the night. Here also groups of calypsonians would sometimes gather under the street lights to sing their calypso songs. This poem is a celebration of those calypso nights that I recall.

**That Happy Band!**

Standing by the street side
in the evening after nine,
you could hear the calypsonians
belting out calypso rhyme:

> *Engine, engine number nine,*
> *rolling down Chicago line,*
> *hold de light mama, I don't want to fight,*
> *hold de light!*

There, beneath the lamplight on
Santa Domingo Street,
near the clubhouse, I remember,
was one place they used to meet.

Sometimes six or eight of them
in a circle gathered 'round—
some standing, some crouching,
some sitting on the ground,

taking turns as the spirit moved them,
matching verse for verse profound,
at the same time keeping rhythm
in a harmony of sound!

I believed their inspiration
must have had something to do
with whatever they were smoking,
because after a puff or two

one of them would chime right in
like a soloist would on cue,
and each phrase was more amazing
for the words, they rang so true!

Then the other background singers
would echo back the chorus lines;
and soon another and then another
tested their creative minds:

>    *You never know the water*
>    *till de well run dry,*
>    *you never know you mother*
>    *till she close she eye,*

he sang, and the chorus then joined in,
>    *Hold de light, mama,*
>    *I don't want to fight,*
>    *hold de light!*

And then another one would sing,

>    *Dollar bill dem run*
>    *from hand to hand,*
>    *but de young gal run*
>    *from man to man,*

And the chorus followed him,

>    *Hold de light, mama,*
>    *I don't want to fight,*
>    *hold de light!*

And on to the next calypsonian,

*What it is you give*
*is what you get,*
*too many times*
*people forget!*

Then the chorus joined right in and sang,

*Hold de light, mama,*
*I don't want to fight,*
*hold de light!*

So all night it went on and on,

*Whatever goes up*
*it must come down,*
*better keep you feet*
*right here on de ground!*

With the chorus singing right along,

*Hold de light, mama,*
*I don't want to fight,*
*Hold de light!*

With no instruments in sight,
just with rhythm and with tone,
with a cigarette in their hand
and their creativity alone,

they would keep it going all night,
or at least until the policeman
made them take a sudden flight;
but like true calypsonians,

they would sing as they moved on,

*Hold de light, mama,*
*I don't want to fight,*
*Hold de light!*

Here they were, this happy band,
singing sweetly about life!
I said to myself, *On the other hand,*
*what they sang about was not my strife!*

My strife was how I was going to explain
to my parents waiting by the door
the reason for coming home late again,
after I had promised not to do it anymore!

To this day, I still cannot forget
that happy band of six or eight
and their harmonizing that was so great,
nor the licking I got for coming home late!

Dedicated to My Beloved Aunt, Stella Noel Aubert, who, like my mother, Philomene Noel Evans, was born in St. Lucia, French West Indies. The two of them came to Panama together in the early 1900s, married two canal workers, and raised their children while maintaining the closest ties as one extended family in Panama City and the Canal Zone. I had several other aunts, but she was my favorite.

**Auntie Lala's Sonnet**

Whenever Auntie Lala came to call
I loved the way she looked; her braided hair
had few grey strands; sometimes she wore a shawl.
She was near fifty give or take a year
and had the warmest smile this side of Heaven,
the kindest heart, the tenderest disposition;
you never heard her shout, swear, or fuss even,
or speak an angry word or cast derision!

Her voice was sweet and gentle when she spoke—
Its pleasing tones still linger on my ear,
though it is years now since a crippling stroke
silenced her voice that I once loved to hear!
Her spirit's gone, but where she is I know
that Auntie Lala's smiles are still aglow!

In 1949, when I was in my late teens and I was coming home from a visit in Panama City one Sunday night, I was walking along Central Avenue near Santa Ana Church. It was mostly quiet near Santa Ana Park sometime after 9 p.m., and my curiosity was drawn to a solitary, gray-haired old lady who was standing in front of a store, intently gazing at the window display for quite some time. I passed her by quietly and kept on walking toward downtown. Several blocks later, I looked back, and she was still standing before the same showcase gazing at it intently. I later wondered what happened to her, and when I reached home I wrote this poem.

### The Old Lady

An old lady was standing by
a store window along Central,
gazing with such a pensive eye
at something in the glass case there.
Her head was not covered at all
so you could glimpse her snow-white hair!
About her neck, a faded shawl
hung down to keep the fresh air out.
The dress she wore (age cannot spare!)
had been a favorite once, no doubt,
when other eyes had feasted there
and other hearts had been devout!
The old woman stood all alone
for quite a while just looking in—
perhaps she dreamed that she could own
what was beyond her purchasing!
A better sense appealed to me
and told me this could never be!
Why would a tired old lady
desire gloves and jewelry
and white-laced wedding gowns? No, no,
it would not do for her to go
plodding along with trembling feet
in such attire down the street!!

78

But I imagined more than that
and saw a gray-haired, old lady
with gentle features looking back
where the bright flame of youth once shone,
at all her priceless treasures gone!

I used to hear the story of Peter Williams when I was very young.  I don't really know if there ever was a real Peter Williams, but I believed it when I was a boy.  Like most folk tales, it could have been exaggerated a bit, but I believe there was some ounce of truth in it.

### The Legend of Peter Williams

On the Canal Zone long ago
there used to be a legend told
about a villain, or hero,
depending on whom you might poll!

Peter Williams, bandit so-called,
stole from the rich and gave to the poor!
Many old-timers still recall
his escapades that are folklore!

Out of shadows he would appear,
loathing barriers in every place,
piercing walls like they were not there,
and vanishing without a trace!

Despite steel bolts and armed police
stark terror ruled some neighborhoods!
The traps they set did not decrease
his crimes for Peter still came good!

'Twas said he studied necromancy,
that he was master of the black art!
No one, but no one, knew the mystery—
how to catch him in the light nor dark,

'cept one friend, Connor, who knew his weakness
and told Patrolman Walters, who
laid wait him one night in the darkness,
and shot poor Peter through and through!

*A silver bullet!* was what he told him,
*A silver bullet, aim for his heart!!*
or else they never would have stopped him;
they shot him down dead in the dark!

He stole from the rich and gave to the poor,
so says the legend of Peter Williams;
he stole from the rich and gave to the poor.
Hurrah for Peter Williams!

When I attended La Boca Normal School, La
Boca, Canal Zone, in the summer of 1947 one of my
classmates, Mola Alphonse, invited some of us to
spend our summer vacation at her parents' home in
Bocas Town, Bocas Del Toro, Republic of Panama.
The Reverend and Mrs. Alphonse were the finest
hosts you could ask for, and their family, including
Mola, made our stay very enjoyable and
entertaining. In the evenings after supper, we spent
the time telling stories and playing social games like
musical chairs, charade, and Pictionary. On a typical
day, we visited friends of the Alphonses or went to
the beach for a swim, or visited the slaughterhouse
where they butchered cows and giant turtles—
turtles and turtle eggs were part of the staple diet
on the island.

While we were in Bocas Town, one
adventure that I will never forget was a journey we
made by sea with the Reverend to visit an island
called Cusapin, which led me to write this poem.

**Bocas to Cusapin**

One night I heard the angry roar
of breakers on a far-off shore
and thought, when I heard it repeat,
a maddened mass of monsters' feet
were trampling on some distant turf
their song of triumph o'er the earth;
but I was told the following day
this was the Caribbean's way.

The morn was bright! With golden rays
Heaven seemed pleased to give her praise
to those who challenge fearlessly
the Caribbean's raging sea.
We were a brave and lively crew,
and for that reason we would do
to wrestle danger anywhere,
for danger thrives only on fear.
Our captain was a gifted man
upon whom God had laid a hand

82

and made him gentle, yet instilled
in him a wondrous, granite will.
He was a man to brave a storm
a hundred times and face no harm,
because his heart was pure and warm,
and he possessed a heavenly charm.

Next to the captain stood a man
who sailed for years the Caribbean.
Although it hardly seemed to show,
by watching him you came to know,
to him danger was not remote,
was not a childish, harmless joke.
He watched the sea with cautious eyes
and only spoke words that were wise!
He watched the pipes continuously;
he watched the gauges—why shouldn't he?
If he should every detail note,
he was the owner of the boat.

The rest of us, less seaworthy,
placed our lives way out at sea
within the hands of those two men
and gave our confidence to them.
Five ladies came along, six men,
and in our midst were two children
making the sum thirteen in all,
an easy number to recall.

We sailed from Bocas at sunrise
with fair weather and sunny skies.
It must have been two hours or three,
when we passed Zapatilla's Key,
which is a kind of beach resort
that everybody raved about.
It was a pretty sight to see
with light brown sand touching the sea,
with milk-white waves washing the sands
and great green palms waving their hands.
We sailed a while o'er calm blue seas
refreshed by fragrant ocean breeze.
Sometimes we climbed our launch for fun
and basked there in the morning sun.

The skies above were very clear—
a crystal dome spread everywhere
whose vastness made you feel aware
how miniscule we are down here!

At last we saw the channel's mouth,
the rough and roaring channel's mouth
that guards the shores of Cusapin!
It was not easy piloting!
Although the sea seemed somewhat mild
and might have settled down awhile
to let us by, our pace was slow
for danger threatened from below
where there were shoals and rocks to pass
and dangerous reefs that could hold fast,
if we had not a captain who
always knew just what he should do.
At last we reached Cusapin's shore,
happy for now danger was o'er.

At Cusapin our Indian hosts
were warm and friendlier than most!
We learned that in these island parts
our own captain had won their hearts:
Here in these unspoiled, untamed lands
he lived among the indians,
poured out his faith and love among
their tribe and learned to speak their tongue,
then studying every vocal sound,

he coded each and wrote it down—
that way their alphabet was born;
he gave their language written form,
then taught them how to read and write
the tongue that is their own birthright!
For all this you can see why then
they honored him among all men
and poured their hearts with love when we
arrived that day across the sea.
They gathered in a little schoolhouse
to welcome and to entertain us.

They sang songs in their native tongue
and in Spanish we sang along.

We went among the tribe that evening
with our captain, visiting.
It was a marvelous thing to see
how he was natural as can be
speaking freely in their strange tongue
while we sat 'mongst them on the ground.
The rest of us spoke not a word
but smiled and made signs when offered
a native drink or piece of meat.
It pleased our hosts to see us eat;
and though their tastes were somewhat different
than our own we were content.
When night came, we retired early;
the school was our dormitory.

We slept with moderate success
surrounded by the wilderness!
There were no sounds except the trees
dancing and flapping in the breeze,
or now and then a creature's shriek
that broke the silence of our sleep!
Two nights we slept in Cusapin
and would have stayed there longer when
the signs of storm clouds far away
hastened the end of our stay.

We packed our things and all was set
to make the journey homeward; yet,
what joy we shared should be reserved
until good fortune had been served!
We said farewell to our hosts
and started for the rugged coast.
Downhill we climbed towards the shore,
heading for Bocas Town once more.
We boarded our waiting craft
and waved goodbye standing abaft.
Our friends waved back as we set sail
before the far approaching gale.
Our launch passed by the dangerous shoals,
and once again our mortal souls

were in the hands of him who steered.
As yet, there wasn't one that feared
when we cruised through the channel's jaws,
though one slight swerve, or one slight slip
would be enough to keel our ship!

Yet fear we should—we had good reason
though courage seemed to be in season!
As we cruised through the channel's mouth,
the sea turned rough and wild about!
Towards each shore the banks we saw
would fill the bravest heart with awe!
The waters dashed in angry tones
against the banks of massive stones!
If anything were thrown that far,
it surely would be rent ajar!
And in the midst of lurking death,
under the pressing strain at length
our steering gear broke from its place!
We swerved! We reeled! But not a face
showed panic for our captain's will
strengthened the crew's—we still
confided all our hearts, our trust
in him, and he was worthy thus.
Our launch was swerving t'wards the rocks,
while four hands strove, before the shock
had pierced our minds, to fix the gear
and thwart the greedy claws of fear!
There was no time at all to spare
if we would foil disaster's snare;
so fev'rishly worked those men
to right our swerving boat again.
I watched those hands move swiftly there;
I watched those eyes that showed no fear,
only the look that strong men wear
who draw from inner strength put there.
Then, as the gear was fixed at last
and his hands turned from their grim task,
our captain rose, retrieved the wheel—
and smiled and said, *There lies Bluefield!*

We stayed awhile
at Bluefield Isle
before we sailed for home again.
We turned around a little bend
and anchored our boat once more
while some of us went off to shore.
At Bluefield Isle, there was no pier
and little pangas standing near
were used to carry us across
the shallow water filled with moss.
'Twas then one lady in our group
had lost her footing, slipped and (oop!)
fell right into the sloppy sea,
and it was quite a sight to see:
She was imperially tall
and she fell in head first of all,
but was not hurt or scratched at all
though slightly shaken in her fall!
Her pleasant disposition helped
to ease much of the tension felt;
we needed no more accidents
after the channel incident!

It was near nightfall when we sailed
from Bluefield—there was never a gale
as if the elements now knew
they found a match in our crew!
The sea was calm, the moon shone down
as we sailed into Bocas Town.

Written and dedicated to my father,
Cornelius R. Evans, while in Rio Abajo, Panama,
1961—the year of his departure.

### Song of My Father

I used to see him often
hold his hurts deep down inside
as if this life could do no more
than was already done!
He'd sometimes sit reflecting
on how the cards were dealt him,
on things past and to come.
He was tired—his battered body
that was once so full and strong
had been beaten by relentless
storms and tempests, years of strife.

Just to look upon his features,
you knew the pain he felt,
knew the suffering he endured.
There were wrinkles in his face
And a sadness in his eyes!
There were calluses in his hands.
He bore scars seen and unseen
and wounds time can't erase!

In despair, I watched my father,
no match for this harsh world,
though he knew to laugh and sing
and love with all his heart,
but what good as shields are these
against inhuman strife
when the strength of limb and loin
can no more bear the brutal sting?

I looked upon my father,
at the shadow he became
of his former self and stature.
He turned feeble, weak and sad
till it touched me to my bones,
till the tears welled up inside!
Yes, I shed tears when I saw him

lying there upon his bed
knowing the drumbeats soon would end,
knowing that he could fight no more
so terrible and so resolute a foe!

Though I shed tears for my father,
I rejoiced for him also,
for he played the hand given to him
in the best way that he knew,
and at last for him the strife was o'er!
Yet if there is any justice,
not in this world but the next,
I am sure he has a blessing
for each scar in life he bore!

*Rio Abajo, August, 1989, written and delivered on the day my mother was put to her final rest—may she rest in peace!*

### Tell Me a Song to Sing

What shall a pierced heart sing?
What can two feeble lips say?
Tell me a song to sing;
tell me the words to say
to take away the grief
when a mother's eyes are closed!
O if I could sing what it means,
or if I could speak how it feels,
I would cause the angels to weep
and the grave to relinquish its claim!

If we think that the mind can forsake
what the heart had enshrined long ago,
let that day for anyone come
when one's mother's eyes are closed!
Then the floodgates are opened wide,
and it matters not how we have grown,
or it matters not where we have been.
There's a bond that can never break,
the dearest and first bond of all:
A mother's love that knows no bounds,
that reaches deep down in our souls!

O to look on my mother's face
while she lay in her final rest,
and to think of my life that she gave,
and of all of her love that was mine,
and to think of her gentle hands,
of her self-sacrificing ways,
and of all that she did just for me
that I never could repay—
it is too much, too much for words,
and too great a debt to bear!

Yet, if somehow she could hear my words
from the place where her spirit has gone,
may she hear then this simple phrase:
That her love was not given in vain,
that her toil, tears, and sweat through the years
are the edifice that brightens my days,
and that she shall forever remain
enshrined in my heart and my prayers!

This poem is dedicated to all mothers and fathers, but especially those of my childhood.

## In Memoriam

They smile no more!
No more their lively themes shall split the air!
No more their voices ring and laughter swell!
Yet only yesterday their linens hung on lines to dry,
when they who smile no more stood by
and watched their little tots
rolling and frolicking in the grass;
and as they stood, friends stopped who, passing by,
had lighter mail to share!
They seemed eternal then as their sweet laughter
sounded in the cool, fresh air!

They sing no more!
No more their lullabies and joyful praise!
No more their gentle chides and sweet reprieves!
No more their kind and loving ways!
No more their proud and happy faces,
as when they saw their offspring off to school,
acting in plays or making speeches!
Yet only yesterday
the world was young and they were gay
and clouds and plagues were far away!

They toil no more!
No more they toil for their dependent ones!
O fallen martyrs!
Yet only yesterday the hungry mouths were fed,
the sick were tended by their hands,
and little shirts were sewn and trousers patched!
Just yesterday
their hands had shown with skill the way to use
familiar tools, and many eyes had watched
and learned from them, then tried to imitate
their skills and practice their examples!

They rise no more!
No more they rise who tucked us into bed at nights

92

and were the last to sleep but first to rise at dawn!
Yet only yesterday they fought adversity for us
and never questioned what it cost;
they healed our wounds and succored us
when we had tripped before life's scars had formed,
and shared our first joys from which all other joys
have come,
wherein we learned the meaning why we strive!
And only yesterday
when we were still not weaned,
they shared our first tears and revealed to us
a wisdom that shall last forever!

They strive no more!
No more they strive who sat in church
and sang sweet hymns and showed the way
and brought new Christians to the fold,
walked down the aisles
and stopped outside awhile with friends,
life full upon their faces!
Just yesterday they made the home at Christmas gay
when, weeks before, they busied with the cleaning:
they polished chairs and painted stoves,
sewed new blinds, baked spiced cakes and told us all
what jobs to do!
And when they said, over the dinner table,
*We thank Thee, Lord,* just being there
their presence added to the bounties spread!
Just yesterday!

O dreaded Death!
O soulless Death! Gloat not as if in victory,
for roots go deep that bind a tree
that bears the fruits that bring forth seeds!
O memory of them who smile no more!

Death touched their flesh
but not their hopes, their dreams, their prayers,
their joys!
Is not a tree embodied in its seeds
that grow and blossom in the sun?
Then Death, sing not a victory song,

for they're not vanquished whom you touched!
They live again,
and share again good fellowship with friends
and neighbors!
O fickle Death! O simple Death!
So long as seeds from seeds shall live,
then they who smile no more shall never die!

Nostalgia keeps taking me back to the town that is no more, my birthplace, La Boca, Canal Zone. The land may still exist, but what is there today is not the same town that we once knew; that town has vanished forever with its history, its drama, and its people, except in memory. Some of my nostalgia I have tried to express here in this poem, as well as in an earlier poem called *Song of La Boca*.

### In the Little Town Where I Am From

In the little town where I am from,
where many years ago,
near by the sea in the tropic sun
children scampered to and fro,
things were not like what they are now—
our town has changed somehow!

In the little town where I was born,
so many years ago,
I remember five o'clock every morn
you could hear the roosters crow!
Some people left home on time owing
a debt to chanticleer's crowing!

During the day while men were working,
and the town seemed desolate,
housewives were busy doing everything
to keep the household straight:
Cleaning, washing, mending, cooking,
praying, economizing!

At three o'clock, silence was broken
when the town with shouting came alive
as a crowd of jubilant schoolchildren
let you know school dismissal had arrived!
And one hour later when the *corchy* blew,
the workmen's workday was through!

On their days off, some men spent their time
building boats, making furniture,
tin stoves and crafts of every kind,
tailoring, gardening, and what leisure
was left, playing dominoes,
or recounting their triumphs and woes!

In the little town where I am from,
where many years ago
near by the sea in the tropic sun
we had scampered to and fro,
things were not like what they are now—
our town has changed somehow!

In the days gone by, when the boys and I
sought adventure, we were up at four,
and out through the town we'd go tramping by,
Some five, ten, fifteen or more
with sticks, toy rifles and sling shots, of course,
and the wilderness path calling to us.

Upon our return from our wilderness trek,
our trophies were few to brag of,
except for bee stings, scratches and a greater respect
for nature and the creatures thereof!
If lucky, we bagged a snake on the run
or a lizard with our sling shots and toy guns!

When we tired of hunting, we turned to the sea
at the mouth of the Great Canal
near the shores where our little town used to be,
where we reveled in the sights one and all,
and we swam in the waters like fishes of the sea,
like creatures born of the sea!

Besides swimming we fished on the piers, barges,
too,
and ate what we caught from the sea.
except for blowfishes and catfishes, quite a few,
that we often threw back to the sea;
fish graced our plates—baked, fried or stewed—
and was a most tasty food!

Of course in the ocean there were dangers and risks,
which we came to know only too well,
for we lost a companion whom we dearly missed
when dreadful King Neptune played his death knell.
We learned from it, yet despite tragedy,
never lost our love for the sea!

In the little town where I am from,
how we played between houses, on the school ground,
in the streets, on the sidewalks up and down
and, if rain, in the cellars, all year round!
There was always a sport to be found
by the boys and girls in our town!

On festive occasions, holidays to be sure,
there were picnics and sporting events
and parades that were colorful, entertaining to the
core.
Afterward there'd be gatherings, lots of food and
drinks,
like the Labor Day fetes on La Boca ball ground
that attracted everyone in our town!

'Twas a joy in those times to see grownups happy,
so nice and generous as a rule!
How we loved holidays, not just the festivity,
but because of the days off from school,
which meant three- or four-day weekends to play
all the games we loved and have our way.

But life was not all about play and games
where grown-ups and parents were concerned!
There were times to care for the sick and lame,
and to share the little they had earned
with those less fortunate who lived in our town,
and to treat their neighbor's plight as their own!

If ever there was a crisis there,
everyone would lend his or her skill,
and healers and midwives would volunteer!
It was like one collective will

that rose to the challenge when crises occurred,
and the whole town responded when they heard.

The wealth of our town was not currency,
for we were not rich whatsoever!
It was the will and the heart and the charity
of the people that were priceless; moreover,
sometimes I think that through poverty
God brings out the best in humanity!

In the little town where I am from—
you could not imagine the tranquility
in its prime when it seemed like no one
even thought that someday it would cease to be,
least of all youth not yet in their prime
who saw just one day at a time!

I grieve for what happened to our town
that used to exist by the sea!
All the houses—they have torn them down;
they rooted up every coconut tree,
and removed every sidewalk we once walked on
and the church where I made first Communion!

The men and the women who were parents then,
who toiled hard for the little that they owned,
must have said to themselves time and time again
when they sensed the fate of our town,
*What will become of the children we birthed?*
*God preserve them, we pray, on this earth!*

In the little town where I am from,
where many years ago,
near by the sea in the tropic sun
boys and girls scampered to and fro,
they have all disappeared, all the people, I fear,
like they never existed there!

**Requiem to Songs of My Youth**

When hearts were young and eager,
when joy was first in bloom,
Time the relentless sealer
primed slower than her loom!

When hearts were young and eager,
causes noble and true,
O how a wistful dreamer
laughed at the chilling dew!

Those were the days when the tempest
only in name did unfold;
power of the rose was the mightiest;
life was a pliable whole!

Dreams, they were never disaster;
Love was a virgin crusade;
Time was a toy, not a master;
Truth was a beautiful maid.

But then the heart grew older,
wrestled the wind and the rain,
and songs that once were bolder
paled in the distant plain.

Sound a salute to their memory;
Time, you have triumphed again;
bury the songs in your valley;
sing them a requiem!

# PART I I :  STORIES

# The Stories of Three Diggers

## Egbert Cleveland Leslie

As we climbed a steep path in Pueblo Nuevo, I grew tired and paused to catch my breath. He turned and said, "Am I going too fast, son?" I looked at this ageless wonder, this soon-to-be centenarian who had worked in the pits of Culebra, the swamps of Matachin, Bas Obispo, Gorgona, Rio Grande, San Pablo and Las Cascadas when the *Big Ditch* was just earth and rock long before I was born, and I could not believe he was ninety-four years old.

I smiled, full of wonder and affection, and continued up the path trying to keep up with him. I reflected as we walked side by side, "Mr. Egbert Cleveland Leslie, you are a priceless, living treasure!"

We reached the top of the hill and kept walking along the side of the road. We must have walked about a mile when the old man stopped and said to me, "This is where I live!" Even at that, we still had to walk up another steep incline from the roadside to the steps of his house, which stood high off the ground on very tall pillars. We had to climb two tall flights of stairs before we finally reached the front door. I was relieved when we got there, but I was also amazed to see how a well-preserved ninety-four-year-old could get around with so much ease.

We sat in the living room, which was kept immaculately neat. There was a sofa, a center table, a vanity filled with crystals, several large-size framed portraits of people (most of whom are no longer with us), a picture of an old Canal Zone town dating back to 1910, a telephone, a side table, and a radio. I told Mr. Leslie I was fascinated with the life and times of the construction era and couldn't wait to hear him tell me about some of his experiences during that time. As eager as I was to hear, he was just as eager to relate his story. He began the following account:

"I was born on November 12, 1888 on the island of Dominica. I came to Panama in 1907 at the age of nineteen, accompanied by my uncle. It was easy then for a youngster of my age to find work in the Canal, especially since I had some schooling, so it wasn't long before I started working as a checker, checking steam shovel output in the Canal—how many cars of dirt they loaded each hour, each day, etc. I received thirteen cents an hour and did this type of work for one year when I became a switchman diverting dump trains from one track to another. I worked in a tower where I received orders from the yard office for clearances around a curve and would switch the tracks. I also was a brakeman for the Central Division until 1910 when I went to work for the Pacific Division in Balboa during the construction of the Pedro Miguel locks. I worked there also as a tower man and a dispatcher for trains coming from and going into the *Cut* until 1912 when I went to work on the labor trains that hauled working people from Panama, Guachapli side, down to Pedro Miguel locks. I was paid thirteen cents an hour, fourteen hours a day. I kept this job until water went into the Canal in 1913."

As he spoke of the past, I tried to visualize what it was like. The only images I had of the construction era were those my father (who is deceased) once told me about when I was a boy, or what I had seen in old photographs of the diggers, but to hear a digger describe it was really a special experience! He must have read my thoughts as he continued:

"Where living conditions were concerned, when I lived and worked in Culebra in 1912, quarters for *silver employees* were shacks that were rough and shoddy. Services inside the quarters were a thing unknown. You had to go out in the yard to an outhouse or community bathroom. Single men lived in camps! In the camps there were about forty bunks in each building, one per person, and a mess kitchen for workers. You were issued tickets worth twenty-seven cents, which were deducted by payroll. With that, you could get coffee and cereal in the morning, and at dinnertime a mass production slop for a meal. A policeman and a watchman stood by to keep order day and night and to make sure you were there legally and had your mess ticket and work papers. In those days, you worked six days a week, and there were no social activities except in the camp where you played cards and dominoes up to nine o'clock. There were a few churches like the Episcopal, the Methodist, the Baptist. There were no roads anywhere. There weren't even any sidewalks! Except that in the white neighborhoods they built boardwalks, but in the black neighborhoods you had to trek in the mud! The only transportation was the railroad, or you walked most of the time you had to go somewhere."

I was very engrossed in his account, and I wanted to know more about how the workers were treated. Again he read my mind.

"Silver workers had no labor organizations, no pension, no disability, none of that, nor any rights or means of protection against unfair treatment; and when you got too old to work, you were superannuated—that means, given a clearance and let go with not even a dime to show!" At that moment my eye caught a photograph on the wall that must be at least seventy years old! There were several gentlemen depicted, and I saw a faint banner with the words *Panama Canal West Indian Employees Association*. I politely interrupted him and asked who those gentlemen were. He pointed to the distinguished-looking man seated and said, "Why, that is Samuel Horton White himself, the leader of the P.C.W.I.E.A.! And this gentleman standing over him is Mr. Graham Lewis; this is Mr. Noel Dalby; this is Mr. W.C. King, and Mr. V. Morrison and you must know who this gentleman is." He pointed to a young man standing at the left behind Mr. White.

"Why, of course," I replied, "That young, handsome, serious gentleman is you, sir!"

He chuckled a bit as he acknowledged by answering with a headshake; then he spoke again.

"You know, in the twenties and thirties the Americans started to take applications from all who wanted to repatriate to the West Indies, passage free. Those first West Indians who went received no money, no pensions! They were sent home with nothing! Many didn't survive for long after they landed. Then the government started giving them, after they were on the boat, $25.00 for the ex-worker, $25.00 for his wife, and $10.00 for each child up to five children. With that, the government washed its hands of them—can you imagine! I don't need to tell you what hardships faced them later when they reached home, and the $50.00 or $60.00 was used up!

"Thanks to the The Panama Canal West Indian Employees Association (P.C.W.I.E.A.) and Mr. Sam White, who fought to change conditions, after a long struggle Congress granted the first disability relief—a dollar a year, up to twenty-five dollars maximum—for otherwise superannuated workers. Some West Indians didn't want the label *disability*, which was only a hardship dispensation. And not everyone qualified for it. For instance, they sent government employees to your home to check on what property you had and deducted from disability according to your possessions—and you better not have any money in the bank! You wouldn't get a nickel!"

As he said that, I thought about Mr. P.S. Martin, an English teacher who worked over forty years for the Panama Canal Zone Colored Schools and had gotten too old to work. He applied for disability—there was no pension at the time. It was said that because he had managed to save $10,000 in the bank over the forty years he worked for the P.C.Z., they denied him any relief. Said he was too rich! He got nothing as a result.

It was getting late, and I could see that Mr. Leslie was a bit tired, although he tried not to show it. So, in a way, I was glad when the housekeeper called from the kitchen and told him that it was time to eat. He asked me if I wished to stay for dinner, but I politely told him I had another visit to make and could not stay. However, I had enjoyed immensely the time I spent with him, and if it were all right with him I would come back another time and visit with him again. He insisted that I do so and very soon. With that I said farewell, and left with anticipation of seeing and talking with my ageless friend again.

It was several years ago in the summer of 1982 when I first met Mr. Leslie. Since then I had returned to the U.S. and was unable to visit him again. About two years ago, 1985, in a conversation with a friend who also knew Mr. Leslie, I happened to mention that I was looking forward to visiting him again on my next trip to Panama. My friend informed me, "I am very sorry you will not be able to do so, because Mr. Leslie, who was critically injured in an accident, died a few months ago!"

"What! Mr. Leslie dead?"

"Yes, he was crossing the street in Pueblo Nuevo one morning, and a truck struck him, seriously injuring him. He was bedridden for a while and couldn't move or speak. A month later he died!"

A dreadful sadness filled the pit of my stomach at the news of Mr. Leslie's death, and I reflected once more on the scene many summers ago with him climbing the hills of Pueblo Nuevo while taking his daily strolls. Infirmity and old age could not stop him, though. It had to take a freak accident and an old truck on a Pueblo Nuevo road! Mr. Egbert Cleveland Leslie, however, in my memory, will always be a priceless treasure.

## Herman Thompson

Herman Thompson was a Panama Canal construction worker disabled since 1964 when he suffered broken ribs and hips while employed by the U.S. Army on the Canal Zone. He retired in 1964 on $80 a month disability and no hospitalization benefits. He lived on Q Street, Caledonia, in Panama City.

When I was in Panama during the summer of 1982, I heard he was bedridden and was unable to attend a celebration given for the surviving diggers, so I went to see him. I remember looking around at the small, shabby, cluttered room where this eighty-nine-year-old man lived. The floors squeaked; a wash basin sat on the table; there was no bathroom or sink—a community bathroom was down the hall. He was very poor and in need of proper care. I felt moved by his plight even as he began to speak:

"They came in here last month (they meaning burglars) and they went through the little place I have with all my papers and a few hundred dollars, and gone with it; so the papers which I had was to take to the government—it's all gone! I have to see how I can start over. It's going to take a long time before the government can replace them 'cause all the Canal Zone records are in the U.S. Government archives in the States somewhere. But anyway, you don't want to hear the troubles of an old man. You say you want to know about the digging of the Panama Canal. I can tell you, yes, I worked in the Canal, dug the Canal. I can tell you about the hardships, the terrible accidents and the slides! Some mornings you got up and the earth came from underneath and raised right up, turned over railroad cars and everything, and we had to go down there and help clear it up. It was hard in those days. But let me begin my account from around the year 1909 if you will bear with me. Let me see now!

"I, Herman Thompson, came here from Manchester, Jamaica as a boy with my brother in 1909 and started to work for the Panama Canal almost immediately, doing odd jobs in the field such as a water boy, messenger, helper, digger, and wireman under the administration of Colonel Goethals, Major Gaillard, Colonel Russo and Colonel Crabtree. One of the foremen taught me how to operate dynamite. Let me tell you how I became a wireman setting off blasting powder in Culebra.

"One morning I was told to catch the next labor train to Culebra because they were short of diggers and helpers. When I got there, it was all swamp in the great big hole they called *snake hole*. Men were on the hill, men were at the bottom manning drills or shoveling dirt and rocks in places where the steam shovel couldn't reach. Others were boring holes for dynamite. The foreman stayed up on the hill overseeing the work from afar.

"A *gallego* was working as wireman placing sticks of dynamite in the holes and hooking up the wire charges. One day, just before noon, they were laying a charge, and the gallego set the dynamite in the hole and hooked up the wire. The all-clear signal sounded, the flagman waved the red flag to the switchman who pumped the charge box to set off the blast—but nothing happened! Damned mad because he thought he hadn't set the charge right, the *gallego* recklessly raced down to the hole to hook up the dynamite right this time. As he got to the hole, an explosion rocked Culebra for miles and miles. All I saw was a head flying in one direction, a hand in another direction and later, pieces of flesh scattered all over the place. It was terrible! Terrible!

"In those days, your life wasn't worth much at the construction site. Men were dying every day from slides, dynamite blasts, malaria, etc. Sometimes when the steam shovel dug up the earth, it would set off a charge, killing workers like flies. So, when the blast killed the *gallego*, work went on as if nothing had happened. Anyway, after lunch that same day, the foreman asked me if I wanted to

108

be the new wireman. You might say I was crazy to take the job, but it meant a four-cent raise to fourteen cents an hour and a chance to work fourteen hours a day, which was damned good wages for any silver worker. I stayed in that job, in one piece, until 1913, when water went into the Canal.

"To this day, I remember when they let the water into the Canal—October 13, 1913. They had cleared out all the towns in and near the *big ditch* where a lot of our people lived—Empire, Bas Obispo, Gorgona, Las Cascadas, Matachin, San Pablo, Bayala Mona, all were going to be at the bottom of the Canal after that day. Clark G. Thompson and I wired the dikes, and the blast was set off by remote control all the way from Washington, D.C. President Woodrow Wilson made a big speech and touched it off by pushing a red button in the White House. Millions of tons of water went rushing into the Canal that day when the Pacific joined the Atlantic for the first time in the history of the world. That's a day West Indians should be proud of, because our labor built the Panama Canal!"

After a little pause, he asked me to reach a package on the table. He took out some pictures to show me—of the time when he was young and of scenes of Culebra Cut; he also showed me several letters he had written to the Canal Zone government seeking to obtain medical benefits and hospital privileges so he could be properly cared for in Gorgas Hospital. He said:

"They turned me down because they claim I retired from the U.S. Army and not the Panama Canal government, but this is not fair, because they are the same U.S. business, and I worked for these people all my life—forty-four years for the Panama Canal government and the last ten years for the U.S. Army—and I was hurt on the job, which is why I was disabled. I have to buy my medicines out of pocket, and I can't afford to pay for private hospital treatment. That's why I am here. But I want to thank you anyhow for coming to see me. I don't want charity, only what's fair, that's all!"

The pride rose in his aging face as he spoke, and I watched, knowing that, somehow, I would always remember the look in his eyes. Before I left him, I placed an envelope on the table with some money as a gift. I tried to be diplomatic because I knew he needed the money. As I said goodbye, I wondered how many other old timers who dug the canal suffered the same fate as he did.

## Reuben Gallimore

He lived in Chorillo, Republic of Panama, across from Fourth of July Avenue in a small apartment where I visited him in 1982. I heard recently that he might have been a casualty of the U.S. army invasion of 1989 when a lot of civilians were killed. I can't verify it, though; I only know that he is no longer with us, and I am gratified that I had the opportunity to visit him before he passed. Here is his story.

"I was born in Culebra in 1896 when Panama was still part of *Old Columbia*. Culebra then was part of what was called *down the lines*, which consisted of Empire, Culebra, Las Cascadas, Bas Obispo, Gorgona, Matachin, etc. I was a little boy, seven years old, when Panama got its independence from Columbia, and the Americans took over the building of the canal. In 1910, about six years after the canal construction was begun, when I was only fourteen years old, I started to work as a *pinche* (water boy). I advanced as time went by until eventually I became a storehouse clerk working in Balboa, C.Z. in 1915. I stayed there until I retired in 1961.

"During the time I worked in Cucaracha, Rio Grande, Gaillard Cut and all up and down the lines as a water boy, messenger, and helper, I saw firsthand how dangerous it was on the construction sites. When they were blasting dynamite and the whistle sounded, if the men didn't move fast enough, they were blown to bits! Sometimes there would be terrible landslides that covered up men and steam shovels alike. Once, when I was a boy in school, I had an experience I will never forget. I was coming home from school, and they had a place in Culebra they called *French Dump*. I was just going through French Dump when I heard an explosion. There was a powder magazine about a hundred feet from the French Dump. I saw a man's head blown up right through the zinc of the magazine roof. That incident made a frightful impression on me as a boy.

111

I couldn't stop talking about it. We lived in those times near the construction sites, and any moment, flying shrapnel and pieces of exploded metal could come through the roof of the house where I slept.

"Living conditions were very poor, of course. The houses were made of wood, and the roofs often leaked. A lot of families were crowded into these living quarters, and the service and bath were outhouses and community bathhouses. But I can say one thing—even though we were very poor, I was happy. I don't know why, but it was so when I was a boy in Culebra Cut.

"As far as benefits were concerned, things are a little better today for me, since I am getting a little pension that helps me. As a Panama Canal Zone retiree, I have hospital privileges, but I am more fortunate than many others who did not get any benefits.

"I gave fifty years service to the Panama Canal warehouse division up to the time I retired in 1961. In my years with the Panama Canal, I had been a water boy, a messenger, a tinsmith helper, and a storehouse clerk. I know that we were poor then, but in my opinion this land was good to us! There was peace and tranquility, and people got along whether you were a Chinaman, Jamaican, Barbadian, Frenchman, or whatever nationality you belong to. Panama is the best country for West Indians, and that's only my opinion."

Today there may only be a few, if any, diggers of the Panama Canal still alive, and if they are, they must be close to or over a hundred years old. I was very fortunate to have personally known some of them. Though the three gentlemen, Messrs. Leslie, Thompson and Gallimore have passed on, I feel that I have lived a part of their lives just by talking with them in the summer of 1982. For that I am thankful.

## Calmetto

The town of La Boca, C. Z. does not exist anymore. It was a little town on the Pacific Coast near the banks of the Panama Canal. It was one of many such towns along the Canal Zone that were built for *silver* employees and their families. It was the town where I was born and spent my boyhood years. There, I went to La Boca Elementary and Junior High School that stood on the very edge or bank overlooking the Pacific Ocean near the entrance to the Panama Canal. La Boca School was a great, long building two stories high, with a bell turret on top, and thirty-six classrooms, four bathrooms, a library, a tailor shop, a carpentry training shop, a large home economics room, and the principal's office on the first floor. The building had a total of approximately 190 windows, five or six per classroom, and from each classroom on the ocean side was a picturesque view of the sea as far as the horizon. We had an excellent view of ships entering and leaving the Canal, and we learned a lot about battleships, cruisers, and tankers by looking out during our breaks and spare time. Sometimes we would be allowed to view from the windows a spectacle like the U.S. fleet in single file entering the Canal from the Pacific Ocean.

In front of the school, facing the town, was a school playground where we played softball and soccer, and when there weren't any games, we flew paper kites. During the butterfly migratory season, we caught butterflies in nets as thousands of them flew overhead.

Behind the school was a steep descent, past a second, narrow ledge where railroad tracks were laid, down to the seashore to a place we called *Calmetto,* which was our beach hideout although it was not a formal beach and was usually not very safe. Many were the times when we *played hookie* from classes to hide out in Calmetto and ended up in the principal's office where we received a severe flogging for it!

Calmetto was the place where I learned to swim, believe it or not, by being tossed into the sea by older boys and given two choices—sink or swim! One might say that wasn't the best method, but, for me and many others, it worked. Of course, there were a few boys my age who had to be rescued after they went down a couple times and looked like they weren't going to make it. It was very unorthodox, to say the least, and may be the reason why some of us developed unorthodox ways of swimming and making an awful big splash! I became very good at floating on my back, and to this day, I'd rather float than swim!

Yet I was good enough at swimming, unorthodox or not, that one day, I remember, three of us took up the challenge to swim to the danger cable and back! It was high tide, and the sea was rough, but there was the danger cable daring us, and our peers calling us cowards if we didn't take up the challenge. Now, let me explain, the danger cable was a high-powered cable that ran on the bottom, near the deeper part of the channel, but there was this four-post structure that stood in the water with a big sign that said, *Danger Cable*. It stood approximately nine hundred yards from our starting point on the shore, and we were supposed to swim to that sign and back.

Melvin, Ashby and I started out for the danger cable posts. Since we knew there was a strong southward current, we started out in a northwest direction to compensate. At first it seemed that our calculations were right, but we underestimated the current, and by the time we reached half the distance, we had drifted too far southward and were too far off line to reach the danger cable. In fact, we now had to swim directly against the current, which would have taken twice the strength we no longer had since we were already tired out, in order to reach our target. We were fighting against the current in dangerous waters and had to forget about the danger cable and think about survival! We knew we were not strong enough to swim back to shore either, but we

114

could not stop swimming. We were about to panic! As we struggled against the current, there was only one chance for survival. There was a pole sticking out of the water about twenty feet south of our position, and, from the looks of things, we had a fifty-fifty chance of making it if we swam northwest as hard as we could, so that by the time we swam thirty feet, the arc would bring us to the pole. Melvin, who was the strongest swimmer, grasped the significance of this and made the greatest effort until he finally reached the pole first. He held onto the pole with one hand and stretched out his other hand to grab us as we went by. If he hadn't done so, neither Ashby nor I would have survived. I grabbed his outstretched hand as I was nearest to him, and when Ashby came by, struggling, I reached out and grabbed his outstretched hand, then we pulled each other to the pole that luckily held our combined weights and withstood the pressure of the current. We held on to that pole for dear life and never moved for hours—at least until the tide subsided low enough that we could swim back to shore.

While we were out there, the other boys on the shore were frantic because they thought we were going to drown. Hours later, when the tide subsided and we regained our strength and courage and swam back to shore, we found out that word had gotten to our parents about our near disaster; but I didn't even mind the tanning I got for putting them through such a scare!

One day in 1972, after being away for almost thirty years, I revisited La Boca, but the house in which I was born, 1071 Gold Street, and the house I later lived in, 1032 Santo Domingo Street facing the school, as well as the church, Saint Theresa, where I made my First Communion, the clubhouse where I frequented and saw many movies upstairs in its theatre when I was a boy, and the ballpark where I saw Vic Greenidge, Pat Scantlebury, Clyde Parrish, and George Griffiths play ball, had all vanished! My brother had warned me, "You're not going to recognize the place, so don't be shocked!"

115

And when I said, "Where's La Boca Elementary School, and the Clubhouse, etc?" he replied, "A lot of the buildings were sold to merchants and crated away or torn down. There's a place called *La Boca Town* in Rio Abajo, Panama, where most of the buildings have been transplanted, and where many retired Panama Canal workers and their families live."

I said, "I wonder where 1071 and 1032 are now, and who is living in our old apartments."

My brother chuckled, "You're a funny one. I'd like to see you find that out! Anyway, as you can see, they have moved out all the *silver* employees and their families and transformed La Boca, C.Z. It is now a plush residential town for U.S. Naval personnel and their families. Instead of tenements, they have private cottages, with private garages, and manicured lawns with sprinklers."

As we drove up to the embankment overlooking the sea, one thing hadn't changed, Calmetto! I asked him to wait fifteen minutes, and I climbed down the banks to have a closer look at my old beach hideout. I went down the rugged path and came to the rocky shore and looked out at the sea. I didn't see the danger cable or the pole that saved my life, but I saw buoys and barges. As I relived the past, I had to take a few flat stones in my hand and fling them over the surface of the water to watch them skip. Yes, this was Calmetto, the place where I learned to *float like a piece of cork and dive like a piece of lead.*

Yes, Calmetto brought back memories. As I stood looking out at the sea, I could remember the time when Glen Isaacs swam from the east bank across the full width of the Canal to the other side, daring current, debris, passing ships and sharks! He was the only person ever to do that. I remembered admiring Matthew Prescott, who could swim the Australian crawl faster than anyone in those days. I always thought he would have swum the Canal like Glen, but he never did.

I could remember, too, the day that Jasper Cox drowned in Calmetto, when he and some

116

companions were fishing on an oil barge, and someone threw a lighted cigarette in the water that set fire to the oil slick. In a panic, they dove into the water under the blazing oil to swim away, but Jasper couldn't clear the flaming inferno, and he drowned. It was a sad day in La Boca as divers went down but couldn't find his body that the current had carried away. It was said that the divers then sent for Mother Lee, the tie-head lady who went out in a little *panga* with a candle in a calabash. She let the boat drift on its own until the candlelight blew out, then she pointed to the place, and that's where the divers found him. Yes, Calmetto brought back memories!

I returned to the car, and as we drove on what used to be called  Martinique Street past where the commissary used to be, I marveled at how the place was transformed—even the trees were different, for there used to be many mango trees and coconut palm trees there in my youth! We drove onto La Boca Road to exit the town, and as we passed by the old ferry road, even that had vanished, for the ferry, too, had vanished—the ferry that connected the east and west banks of the Isthmus; but of course, that was due to progress, as there was a bridge, the Thatcher Bridge, built to connect the east and west shores some time ago, making the ferry obsolete.

Gradually, it seemed to me, all the traces of the life, the towns and the people who lived in the silver towns along the canal were erased from the face of the earth. La Boca was not the only one, nor the first, nor the last. The proof of their existence, though, is in the minds and hearts of many who, like me, still carry their special memories of those long-vanished places.

# Mr. Maximilian

When I was a boy in La Boca, C.Z., Mr. Maximilian used to visit our home occasionally, about once every six months. I believe he would have visited more often, but he had to come from very far. He lived in the country, in the interior of Panama, *over the Ferry* we used to say, about five miles on the west side of the Panama Canal. That was far because he usually walked, although sometimes he took the interior bus on its way from Chiriqui or Chorrera to the city, and it would drop him off near La Boca, and then he would walk from La Boca town limits to our house. He was a skinny man of medium height and dark complexion, elderly, country or earthy-looking, always very plain and simple in attire. I remember he used to smoke a pipe, which he made himself from a section of corncob. The center of the cob was soft; he gouged it out and stuck a tube in the side of it for puffing the smoke. I think he grew his own tobacco, but I am not sure. I liked to watch him puff on his pipe, and sometimes, when the fire was dying down, he would draw frantically on the tube till the tobacco re-ignited, and he could puff more easily to his satisfaction. He and my father and mother were friends from way back, and they all spoke *Patoit*. My mother and he originally came from St. Lucia where they were born and where people speak broken French, called *Patoit*. My father's mother also came from St. Lucia, but my father was born in Panama. On his visits, the three of them had a lot to talk about, especially since Mr. Max was glad to be with company which his solitary life otherwise denied him, and he would sometimes spend the night. How the *Patoit* used to fly then!

Whenever he came, he would always bring a large *crocus* (burlap) bag sometimes filled with chickens (though I don't know how they were still alive), but mostly he would bring produce which he grew on his little farm in the interior. There was always plenty of cocoa, yam, yucca, potatoes, *yampi,* and corn. Mr. Maximilian was one of those

118

men, like my father, who loved the land, the feel of the soil between their fingers, the mystery of nature, and the art of extracting her secrets from her with their strong backs and hands, and patience. They also loved seeing and handling the products of their hard labor, and sharing them with others. Through their efforts, our family had plenty of fresh *earth food,* and we didn't have to buy a lot of groceries. Sometimes when my father reaped his harvest (for he also had a little farm on Far Fan Hill on the West Bank, just across the ferry), he would travel to the interior and take a portion for Mr. Max. Whenever Mr. Max visited, we would give him a lot of provisions like salad oil, kerosene, and rice, that we bought for him since he didn't have commissary privileges. So it was a reciprocal kind of arrangement.

I always liked to watch Mr. Maximilian unload his *crocus* bag like Santa Claus unloading toys at Christmas. I was especially thrilled one day when he came to visit because he brought with him a special small box along with the crocus bag that he had carried over his shoulder. It seemed there was a conspiracy between him and my father to surprise me on my birthday, because in that box was a little puppy, my birthday present. You see, Mr. Max also raised on his farm dogs, cats, and chickens, although I didn't know how he kept them from fighting each other, or the dogs and cats from eating the chickens, but things seemed to work out quite well in that respect between the animals.

This brings me to a very startling story which my father related to us one day about Mr. Max and one of his pet animals—a story that I will never forget. It happened that Mr. Max had a cat he called Missie which, for a long time, he had treated in a special way. She slept in the house in the master bed, she ate when he ate at the same table with him, and she enjoyed a position of privilege in the house. I don't know how cats think, but I am sure this one thought that she was *it,* the princess, the prima donna, the mistress of the household.

119

One day a lady friend came to spend the weekend with Mr. Maximilian. That changed things quite a bit. When they sat down at table to eat, the cat didn't do anything else but jump up on the table to declare her status, and to eat at her place with him like she always used to do. Well, Mr. Max gave her a hell-of-a *box* and knocked her off the table and chased her away. Missie sulked and ran outside, and stayed away from the house till the guest was gone. Then Mr. Max let her back into the house after the lady left. He thought the incident was over, but while he was sleeping that night, the cat jumped on his face, nearly suffocating him! Luckily he awoke and managed to push her away; but she jumped on him again, and grabbed his most private part and almost tore it off! Fortunately he had a gun nearby, which he grabbed and shot the poor jealous thing dead. But still, he had to go to the hospital for treatment. After Missie, he didn't keep another cat on his farm. You can understand why.

Mr. Maximilian, who had neither children nor kin, had given up city life a long time ago to live by himself in the country. He loved his solitary life, and he loved farming, raising animals and chickens, but being alone has its disadvantages. For instance, if he should suddenly take ill, there would be no one there to attend to him, or even call for emergency help. He didn't even have a telephone! It is true that it was his choice to live that way, but the worst possibility is exactly what happened to him one day. He became very ill, and by the time anyone went there to check on him, it was too late! Perhaps it would not have saved his life in any case, if it was his time to go, and perhaps he left this world the way he wanted to; but there seems to be something very wrong, very sad about a person, anyone, passing on with nobody there to pray for them, or hold their hand, or comfort them. He must have thought of this possibility when he chose to live in the wilderness by himself, and I wonder if in his last moments he did not regret it. Nevertheless, I suppose some fatalist might say, why should he, since in nature, life passes everyday and new life takes its place, and who grieves for a fallen sparrow anyhow? But I beg to differ—I think the angels do!

## The Lady in Green

At the railroad station in Colon, Republic of Panama, people were rushing to board the train bound for Panama City. One lady, who walked as if she was totally oblivious to the imminent departure of the train, was in Bryan's way as he was rushing by. He almost knocked her down when he went past her onto the platform. Turning, he apologized, but she gave no indication that she was even affected by the near accident as she ignored him and continued to take her own sweet time. Bryan had paused for only a second and shook his head as he boarded in front of her.

The cars were very crowded, and he had difficulty finding a seat, but, on the verge of giving up, finally he saw one in the rear of the last car. A bit tired, he rested awhile before starting to read a letter he was saving for the moment when he could relax. He had hardly finished the last line when he glanced across the aisle directly diagonal from where he was sitting and saw the lady he had almost bumped into! He had already dismissed her from his mind after the incident; however, now he found himself curious and could not take his eyes away from her. Smooth-complexioned, of light brown skin, somewhat mulatto, modestly attractive in appearance, she could not be older than twenty-five. Her eyes were amber-colored and dreamy. Her soft black hair blew wildly in the wind, and she had a detached gaze and an introspective demeanor that kindled his curiosity! After what seemed like a very long time, he collected his senses, chided himself for being carried away, and spent the rest of the trip answering his letter, later viewing the scenery and thinking about Panama City and home.

The train left Colon Station at four-thirty that Friday evening and arrived in Panama City at exactly six o'clock. "It is good to be back in the city!" he said to himself as he came out of the station and gazed at the seven-story International

122

Hotel, the cafes, the Happy Land night club along Central Avenue, the pedestrians busily tramping up and down, the peddlers on the street, the lottery venders sitting on the curbs with their lottery boards, the policeman directing traffic, the *chivitas* and taxis zooming up and down, honking their horns! Yes, everything was still the same, even the faces in the crowds along the street, some of whom were somber and cold, but the majority were filled with excited laughter. Bryan was standing at a bus stop in front of the Panama Railroad Station building, awaiting transportation to Rio Abajo, when someone brushed against him on the sidewalk. He looked around and saw it was the lady he almost bumped into while boarding the train! He could never forget her face, her well-formed figure, her elegant though casual gait and the green dress that she wore. Perhaps she was repaying him for bumping into her when he boarded the train in Colon! Now he just watched her as she disappeared in the distance, and would have stood there still watching the corner where she turned if a chauffeur hadn't shouted, *"Rio, Rio Abajo!"*

Bryan Weldon, a young man in his mid-twenties, worked in Silver City, C.Z. as a fourth-grade schoolteacher in the public schools, returning home every Friday evening for the weekend. He stayed with relatives during the week in Colon, but every weekend he looked forward to returning home and spending Saturdays and Sundays with his parents, brothers and sister. To him, the weekend was too short as usual. After the Sunday National Lottery had played, he, his parents, his two brothers and sister had an early dinner together, which was hardly finished when it was time to leave home. He took with him a special cake his mother had baked and packed carefully so as not to be damaged, and he rushed off with his traveling bags to catch the Sunday afternoon train heading back to Colon.

Arriving at the Central Avenue station early, he had plenty of time to kill, but fortunately he had brought a couple of magazines along, which he began to read before the train left the station. He was engrossed in the pages of a magazine when the last warning bell sounded signaling the train's departure, and his concentration was broken by the last-minute rush of passengers who were boarding and trying to find comfortable seats, causing Bryan to postpone reading until the train had left the city, until everything had quieted down and they were somewhere out in the countryside. He looked around and acknowledged greetings from passengers he knew. Everyone was smartly dressed! The car was filled with the odor of perfume, but it was Sunday! On Sunday, everybody wears their Sunday best! After observing almost everyone, he turned to peruse the *Sunday Tribune* he had brought with him, when his glance accidentally fell on a familiar figure in a green dress! He looked again and, to be sure, she was sitting about two seats in front of him. He could barely see her face, but there was no doubt, it was the same soft black hair and mulatto complexion. She was looking through the window in a trance-like gaze like she was far away, the same as before. "What deep philosophical thoughts," he wondered, "could she be contemplating?" The thought went through his mind until he reminded himself that the lady's demeanor and preoccupation were none of his business. After all, if it bothered him so much, and if he wanted to speak to her, why didn't he do something about it and introduce himself to her. The worse that could happen would be that he'd get rejected, and who knew, he might get lucky! He chose not to, and forcing himself to dismiss her from his mind, he started to doze awhile, though somewhat uncomfortably. When he awoke, he found that he had slept all the way to Colon and wasted practically the whole trip. Then, involuntarily, he thought about the lady! He was suddenly filled with the desire to see where she had turned after leaving the train, but she was nowhere in sight when he got off the train, and he chided

124

himself again, "Bryan Weldon, you sentimental fool!"

About two weeks later, it was a Sunday evening and time to return to Colon to start another week at Rainbow City Elementary School. In the back of his mind, he wondered if he would ever see the mysterious lady again. That Sunday evening, Bryan was very late coming from Rio Abajo and were it not for his brother, who brought him down by car at the risk of getting a speeding ticket, he would never have caught the train. They left home at 4:10 p.m. and since they saw that they could not reach Panama station in time, they took a shortcut via the Trans-Isthmian Highway into Currundu and over to Balboa Station, the next stop on the train route. When they got there, Bryan ran about twenty yards and hopped onto the train at great risk! He got to a seat exhausted, and sat semi-delirious for a few minutes before regaining his composure. It was the conductor who revived him when he said, "TICKETS PLEASE! LETS HAVE YOUR TICKETS!"

After paying his fare, he began examining the faces of passengers in the coach, and seeing that he was among strangers, focused his attention on the changing scenery along the countryside. The sky was a bright sunny sky, the trees were fresh with flowers and blossoms, and every bush and herbage lent its share of beauty to the colorful scenery. The marshy waters were crowded with water lilies whose outstretched skirts, each joined to each, formed a great green blanket on which were mounted showy, fragrant flowers. Just past Gamboa Station, all along the route, there were glimpses of the Shagres River. There were lakes and bridges. Sometimes passengers could catch a glimpse of a ship sailing through the Panama Canal en route to the Atlantic Ocean.

The train was passing through Miraflores when Bryan's thoughts ran once more to the lady, and he turned abruptly from the window. Curious and restless, he got up from his seat, took his books and his traveling bag, and started to walk through the coaches. There were three second-class coaches, and it was in the first coach attached to the engine that he saw her at last! Dressed in green, she sat facing the door looking directly at Bryan as he entered the coach, almost as if she was expecting him to walk through the door. As their eyes met for the first time, she smiled at him—a warm, gentle smile! He was moved as he nodded and tried to mutter, "H-h-h-i-i-i!" and staggered toward a seat not far away.

Although she did not speak, her smile spoke for her. Her face was radiant and warm, with a strange quality of inner serenity. She did not seem as distant as the previous times he saw her. He was greatly encouraged. After all, she finally acknowledged him as if she was aware of him all along, and in her own way decided to give him an opening. He sat for ten minutes, reflecting on her smile. When they reached Colon this time, he thought, he would definitely have the courage to make her acquaintance. He would wait until then! Or, perhaps if the person sitting next to her got up, he would have an opportunity. He took another glance at her before opening the pages of a book he had brought with him. She was looking out the window, and her hair was dancing in the wind.

Then he returned to reading his book, *Adventures in American Literature,* and was soon lost in the pages of Edgar Allan Poe's *A Cask of Amontillado.* He finished the story and looked up, but she was not there! How long she had vanished or where she went, he did not know. He assumed that she would soon return, so he waited. Then there was a commotion on the train! The conductor rushed through the aisles. The train came to an abrupt stop with a loud screech, and everyone was excited. Some of the passengers were looking through the window. A crowd of them had gotten off the train and were gathering on the tracks. Out of curiosity, Bryan was hurrying to join them, too, when he heard someone say, "...didn't have a chance...there's nothing anyone can do now!" And as he approached the scene, his heart quickened, then he became slightly numb. What did they mean, "Didn't have a chance?" What was going on? Where was the lady in green? He got off the train and approached the scene like all the other curious people. He tried not to think of the thought that was piercing his consciousness, fearful as it might be, but there was no doubt as he approached the scene whom they were talking about—it was the lady in green!

For a moment, he just stood there on the tracks, awed by the finality of death and the frailty of human existence, and he cursed the hand of fate. In her fall (or leap) from the train, she must have suffered a broken neck and died instantly! Just before they covered her body, he gazed upon her crumpled, lifeless form and could not understand. As he stood there, too emotional and stunned to even move, in his mind he could see her again, gazing intently through the coach window, her frivolous hair in the wind; he remembered her casual gait, her dreamy eyes; and he remembered, too, the last smile anyone would ever see again on her face! Unfortunately, it was only then that Bryan knew what that smile meant. It would take him a long time to forget.

The next evening after supper, as he was perusing the daily newspaper, *The Panama American*, he accidentally came upon an article that said:

Daughter of prominent social figure ...commits suicide on train bound for Colon yesterday. It was revealed that she was returning from one of her weekly secret visits to the San Fernando Clinic in Panama City where she was undergoing tests and preliminary treatment for cancer...She is survived by..."

Bryan could not read any further. He folded the newspaper and went out into the night to walk alone with his thoughts.

## The Contest

Yampy was short and weasel-eyed, and had a slightly large head for his body. He didn't say too much, but, after all, he was a man of action, not of words. As a student, he was unassertive, lazy and poor in his studies and schoolwork, but he was always getting into mischief! Mischief was his second name. Sometimes it seemed that teachers were picking on Yampy, but it was the other way around.

Now, Sharpy was a little taller than Yampy and had a long head with shifty eyes. He was frivolous, simple, always grinning and giggling, easily led, and above all, mischievous and very poor in his studies and schoolwork.

What would a seventh-grade class be without people like Yampy and Sharpy? Dull with a capital D! We took English together, Yampy, Sharpy, myself and two dozen other boys and girls in La Boca Junior High School. P.S., a strict disciplinarian, was our English teacher, and what an English teacher he was! Middle aged, of medium stature, mestizo complexion, of slightly graying hair, he was a serious, gentle, kind church-going, God-fearing man. In the classroom, however, he sometimes displayed another side of his personality that all of his students came to know very well. When he addressed the class about the pitfalls of mischief and laziness, he was very emotional! He was a soft and gentle man until he was provoked by some prankster—he was relentless then! Like Dr. Jekyll who changed to Mr. Hyde, Peter Samuel Martin became a fire breather! It was amazing! He could smell mischief a mile away and would bring his wrath down on all who tempted him by their misconduct. Sometimes I thought he was an exorcist! He seemed to exorcise the devil from his classroom! His was a classroom of law and order, peace and quiet, dedicated learning, hard work interspersed with an occasional quotation from the Bible or a poignant story from classical literature, skillfully dramatized by him. In P.S.'s class no one dared speak out of turn; no one dared come late to class; and no one dared leave without permission before the class was dismissed. I stress these last two points strongly because this story is based on them.

Yampy and Sharpy were very proud of their exploits and were willing to share fame equally until the question arose one day, "Who is the number one mischief-maker in the whole school?" It would have been simple for one of them to say it was the other and settle the matter without a fuss, but neither one was willing. It had to be settled some other way. They finally agreed and decided that the test would be to see who could break one of P.S.'s rules and get away with it! If they went through with this, it would be like going to the gallows; like meeting Death face to face; nothing less than suicide, in effect. It would be better to walk on fire, sleep on nails, or sink to the bottom of the ocean rather than commit a prank in P.S.'s class! Anyway, Yampy and Sharpy were so reckless that it didn't matter!

The contest, then, was based on the test in which each one would break one of P.S.'s rules, and the one that did it (without being caught, mind you) would be declared the Greatest Mischief Maker of All Time. Specifically, Yampy was going to sneak out of P.S.'s class in the middle of a session without asking permission, and without being detected by P.S. Sharpy, in turn, was going to deliberately enter P.S.'s classroom late, in the middle of a session without excuse and without being detected. Both of these were formidable feats!

The day for Yampy's test came. That morning, Sharpy and Yampy met before going to P.S.'s class. I heard Sharpy say to Yampy, "You wouldn't want to add a little bet on the side, would you, Yampy? How about it? How about it?"

"Why not," said Yampy. "But remember, you don't win unless I fail and you succeed."

"And vice versa," retorted Sharpy. "Let's make it a five then, for the winner!"

That afternoon after lunch, we reported to P.S.'s class as usual, on time and ready for work, bright-eyed and bushy-tailed. P.S. was in rare form that day as he taught us about the present, past, and progressive tenses of irregular verbs. He called on us, and we responded individually. Sometimes he had us respond as a group in chorus. When our individual turns came, he would tolerate no mistakes and was hard on those students whom he thought were lazy. I remember it was Luther Franco's turn, and he erred in the conjugation of an irregular verb. What happened then was high drama that kept you on the edge of your seat. P.S. paused for a brief moment—you could hear a pin drop! Poor Luther sat trembling, trying to mumble the right answer to correct his mistake, but it still came out wrong. Then there was a loud sound of P.S.'s book as he closed it with both hands, "whhaaammm," and he addressed himself to Luther:

"Stand up! You'd better stand up! Stand up and let them all see you—see the clown! You'd better not come with any foolishness here! You know why you don't know your lesson? Because you're lazy, that's why! If I had my way with you, I'd feed you verbs for breakfast, verbs for lunch, verbs for dinner till it came out of your pores!"

The drama had every student shaking in his boots and making sure that he or she knew the right answer to the next question should he or she be called upon, because no one wanted to be in Luther's place. By now, I was beginning to think about Yampy and was feeling sorry for him if he should break a rule and get caught; but if there was one thing that Yampy and Sharpy had, it was courage.

The lesson was continuing without further incident after Luther's ordeal and repentance for not studying his homework, and everyone was giving only right answers now. I kept looking around to see when Yampy would make his move, if he didn't change his mind by now, and the next instant he was out of his seat! Yampy was smart. What he did was slip down between the seats and start to crawl around the back of the room toward the far aisle adjacent to the exit. He was going to sneak out, or so he thought! He was crawling on his belly and was halfway down the aisle not more than ten to twelve feet from the door. I looked at P.S., and he was teaching away as if he was completely unaware of Yampy, but I would soon learn otherwise. As Yampy reached within five short steps of the door, P.S. slammed his foot down hard, whhaaammmm!, and pointed toward the place where Yampy crouched in hiding. In a few seconds, P.S. had turned red in the face as if his head were on fire! He stood up, and hurried over toward Yampy. "S-a-a-a-t-t-t-a-a-a-n-n!! he shrieked, "S-a-a-a-t-t-t-a-a-a-n-n! You crawling insect! Vermin of evil! With the foot of Jehovah, I am going to stamp you out! His feet came down hard on the floor again, wwhhhaaarrraaammmmm!!! Great God! I thought it was Yampy's head he had stomped! I thought for sure Yampy was dispatched to the other world; but he was still alive and breathing. P.S. didn't touch him, but Yampy was trembling like a leaf in his tracks—or should I say, on his belly—and he must have thought that it was the end, because the next thing I knew, he was praying on his knees.

"Please Mr. P.S., I won't do it again! Please Mr. P.S..."

I really don't believe P.S. meant to do Yampy any harm, but the drama must have scared Yampy out of his wits. He returned to his seat a shaken mischief-maker.

That evening, Sharpy tried to collect his bet, but he was reminded that he had to succeed first in his test. So the next day he put his plan in motion. P.S.'s class began on time as usual, but without Sharpy, who had gone over to the clubhouse to buy some hot beef patties! He returned as planned halfway through the 11 o'clock class. I saw his head peep through the doorway, showing his inimitable grin! When he thought P.S. wasn't looking, he ducked down low and crawled through the open doorway in an attempt to creep down the adjacent aisle, almost the reverse of the direction that Yampy tried to take the day before. The strangest thing happened that made me think P.S. either had eyes in the back of his head or extrasensory perception. His back was toward the door, and as Sharpy entered, P.S. cried out, "An evil spirit has entered the room! My soul was at peace until an evil spirit just entered this room, but Jehovah will strike him down!" P.S., red with rage, rushed toward the back of the room to cut Sharpy off in his tracks. "B-e-e-l-z-e-b-u-b!" he cried, "L-u-c-i-f-e-r! Stop before I cut you in half with the sword of Jehovah!" And he brought the yardstick in his hand down so hard on the top of one of the desks that it broke into a dozen pieces and missed Sharpy's head by inches. Sharpy felt like crawling into the woodwork rather than face P.S.'s wrath. P.S. pointed to the door screaming, "Out! Out! Creature of darkness! Back to whence you came!" And as P.S. held a book in his hand and raised it menacingly, Sharpy didn't wait for the blow to strike; he ran out of there scared half to death as if a tiger was on his tail. Of course, both he and Yampy never tried anything like that again in P.S.'s class!

As for the outcome of the contest, well, it ended in a tie as far as Yampy and Sharpy were concerned. In fact, their careers as mischief-makers suffered a serious, though not fatal, blow by that arch nemesis of mischief-makers, P.S.M. (Peter Samuel Martin), alias P.S. (for Pepper Sauce).

# The Promoter

The interviewer knew he was a journalist, historian, statesman, ambassador and former tennis star, but she didn't know that he was also a first-class promoter of public events and concerts on a large scale, and that he had helped bring to Panama a number of internationally famous artists back in the forties, such as Marian Andersen, Paul Robeson, Paul Warfield, Tod Duncan. His other achievements were well documented; however, being a great promoter was not something the reporter could trace, so of course, she ventured to find out in an interview she had with George one day.

"George, how did you come to be a promoter? Was this an old ambition or talent of yours that goes a way back?

Usually, it was difficult to get him to talk about anything unless he knew you well, because he was a very private person by nature. When she asked him the question, she thought at first that he didn't hear her, but of course he did. The question seemed to trigger something, however, and for a moment his mind wandered off somewhere.

In fact, George's mind went back forty years to 1924, when he was fourteen and attending teacher Innis' private school in Guachapali, Panama. He was sitting in teacher Innis' class, and being bright, well disciplined, an advanced student, and teacher's favorite, he was given the duty of monitoring the class to see that order prevailed—that is, students kept their mouths shut and remained in their seats whenever Innis left the room. Some people said he was chosen because he loved to *snitch* on the others, but that may not have been the case. Anyway, George always kept accurate notes of who did what when, so that when the teacher returned, he had a complete and accurate account. George performed his duty well, so well in fact, that the other students were gunning for him, especially after teacher Innis, a strict disciplinarian, gave the errant ones several whacks on the open palms of their hands with a hardwood ruler he kept for that purpose.

One evening after school, two of the boys he reported were lay-waiting for him to beat him up, but George got wind of it and went over and asked his friend, *Matty Baby*, whom George made sure he helped with his homework, and never snitched on, to help him out by walking with him to Larry's bus. Larry was a native Barbadian who ran a lucrative bus service taking kids from La Boca to Panama City to school and delivering them safely home afterwards; so, once George was in Larry's bus, he was safe. After school when he came out into the schoolyard, the two boys thought they had him and were about to pounce; but, Matty Baby was right behind George, and he flexed his muscles so that the boys could see, for he had big muscles for his age. He saved poor George's neck that time; but the boys didn't forget, and they didn't give up either. They figured that since he, George, got a strongman to back him up, they were going to get one, too, so they picked the biggest bully in the school who was a little dumb academically, and whom they just called *Willie the Bully*. They figured if they got Matty Baby out of the way by letting Willie beat him up, then they could get to George and *fix his wagon*.

So one day when George was leaving school with his escort, the two boys and Willie were waiting. Willie was much bigger than Matty Baby, and everybody thought it was a mismatch; but Willie didn't have the fists nor the speed of Matty Baby, and he didn't hit as hard! So, of course, Matty Baby made short work of him in front of all the other boys who had gathered to watch. George, of course, felt safe then; but more important, when he looked around and saw the crowd, and the skill of Matty Baby, he said to himself, "Oh no, next time they aren't going to see no free fights, not on their lives!" So he became a matchmaker from that time on, arranging bouts between the bigger boys and his bodyguard, reaping in all the profits.

He would stage the fights in a spacious yard behind the big Muller's Building, in Panama City, a couple of blocks up the street from teacher Innis's schoolhouse. The bouts were clean, one-to-one fist fights, and there were always thirty or more kids crowded around, paying admission of course, shouting from the sidelines as the protagonists settled the score. After a time, nobody wanted to fight Matty Baby, because he was too good, and he was declared the champion of teacher Innis's school. Incidentally, his real name was Leopold Mowatt, and he later became a professional boxer in Panama. Anyway, after Matty Baby, George came to be known by his schoolmates as, among other things, the little promoter who could arrange contests, matches and things.

"George, George, did you hear me?" said the interviewer.

George's presence of mind caught up with him, and he suddenly returned from the past—all of which took only about thirty seconds—with a smile on his face, as he turned towards the interviewer.

"But of course I heard you! As for your question, I always wanted to be a promoter, among other things. I always knew I could be good at it, too!"

And George Westerman, the writer, historian, statesman, ambassador, ex-tennis star, and *promoter* looked at his interviewer and smiled.

"It's time for lunch," he said. "Would you care to join me? I'll tell you all about it over lunch."

She thanked him for the invitation, and as they went off, you could hear them still chatting about a number of subjects: politics, history, sports.

## The Reverend

It was said that before he was called to the ministry, he had an encounter with God! In his youth, he was wild and worldly. He was working as a pilot, operating a motor launch for the United Fruit Company in Panama, when one day he had a near disaster at sea and never thought he would survive. That experience changed his life and led him to convert to the Methodist faith and later become a minister.

His resume would fill a book; however, to elaborate on that is not my intention. I will say, though, he was one of the most gifted and extraordinary persons I have ever met. He had a charm and an ease in dealing with people; he was at home in any circle, and could communicate exceptionally well on all levels. One example of this was the time he was preaching a sermon in Pilon, Panama to simple country people. It was noted that he delivered the sermon in a quaint, peculiar vernacular of the villagers called, *Patoit*. Later that same day, at the Cathedral in Colon, he delivered the same sermon, but in a formal, eloquent language, contrasting that of Pilon. When he was asked why he did that, he replied, "My mission is to communicate and to bring the message to the people. The language that they understand best is the means of doing so." An example of his down-to-earth sense of humor was the time he was giving a sermon and made reference to a commonplace saying that people often used. He said, "There are times when people talk about giving you a 'piece of their mind.' You often hear them say, 'Yes, child, I gave her a piece of my mind, I tell you,' but they don't tell you which piece. Well, any time they say that, you can be sure that it's not the good piece, it's the dirty piece they are giving!" At a wedding he once said, "You shouldn't worry if your partner loves you or not; you should love enough for both of you, that way you'll have no reason whatsoever to get in a jealous rage or domestic quarrel, let alone divorce."

137

My personal contact with the Reverend Ephraim Alphonse took place when I visited his home in the summer of 1947. I was attending La Boca Normal Training School when a group of *Normalites* and myself were invited by the reverend's daughter, Mola Alphonse, who was a classmate of ours, to spend our summer vacation at the home of her parents, who lived on the island of Bocas Del Toro.

About a week after we arrived, the reverend took us on a trip by sea to the remote islands of Cusapin to visit the Guaymi Indians, a once primitive tribe. The night before sailing, as I slept in the home of the Reverend and Mrs. Alphonse, I could hear the roar of the breakers on the far-off shore that sounded like a horde of monsters stampeding on the distant turf. The next day, however, the morning was filled with a golden sunshine like a blessing from Heaven, which was a lovely way to start off our journey.

The sights along the way were beautiful. We passed Zapatilla's Key, a natural beach with light brown sand touching the sea, milk-white waves washing the sands, clear blue-green waters, and great green palm trees waving to us from the shore. Occasionally we saw giant turtles beneath the ocean surface or basking on the shore, and there were beautiful tropical birds of all colors who most certainly appreciated their wilderness paradise.

After four or five hours of pleasurable sailing, we finally reached the channel entrance to the shores of Cusapin. Although the sea seemed mild, we moved cautiously, for danger was always threatening in the form of hidden shoals and pointed rocks and dangerous reefs just below the surface that could spell disaster if we did not have expert hands piloting the boat. Our captain, the reverend, knew these waters like the palm of his hand, and there was no need to be concerned. We got through safely and reached the shores of Cusapin.

We climbed the mountain up to the Indian village where the whole tribe came out to meet us. They were warm and friendly. We learned that in these islands, our captain was revered by the Indians, for it was here, in these unspoiled, untamed lands that he had lived among them for several years, pouring out his faith and love, learning to speak their tongue, studying their vocal sounds, coding each and writing them down. Then he went to work and created an alphabet that gave their language written form, and he taught them how to read and write in their own language for the first time! He created a Guaymi dictionary. (I still have a copy today which he autographed.) He also translated the Bible and many classics into their language—all this today is in the Smithsonian. You can see why, then, the Guaymies honored him greatly and poured out their hearts when we arrived that day across the sea.

They entertained us in a little church house they had built, which we used as our dormitory during our stay. They sang songs in their language and gave recitations. We joined them as best we could, although we did not speak their tongue. Later that evening we visited several Indian families with the reverend. We sat on the grass or on stumps and watched him converse so naturally with them in their tongue. They were eager to offer us food and drink, and though our tastes were somewhat different from theirs, we showed our gratitude for their hospitality. When night came, we slept with moderate success, surrounded, often awakened, by the sounds of the trees dancing and flapping in the breeze and now and then different creatures shrieking in the darkness!

After the second night, there were signs of a storm in the distance, and we decided to leave before it came, because storms in that region were too rough for the uninitiated, which we were. We hurried and packed to make our departure, said goodbye to the Indians and climbed down the mountain, hurrying to cross the channel before it became impassable due to turbulent tides. We boarded our waiting craft and waved to the Indians as we set sail before the fast approaching gale storm. As we were going through the channel, for the first time I realized how dangerous that crossing was! The sea started to get very rough! Between us and the shoreline, there were nothing but huge jagged rocks protruding near the banks. The water started to get choppy! The boat was rocking with the waves, but we were in control—our captain, that is. The water dashed fiercely against the banks of massive stones; if anything were thrown against them with that ferocity, it would have been ripped to pieces! And in the midst of all that lurking danger, under the pressures of the turbulence, in the middle of the channel, our steering mechanism suddenly broke! Needless to say, the boat swerved wildly! It swerved! It reeled at the mercy of the tide. But not a face showed panic! The captain's will strengthened the crew's. He kept us calm, and we trusted him to bring us through! And as the launch tossed and swerved on the verge of capsizing, his hands and the copilot's worked feverishly, before the shock pierced our minds, to fix the gear of the launch that was out of control! I watched those hands move deftly, swiftly, and those eyes that showed no fear—only the look that some men wear who draw strength from deep within. Then—miraculously—somehow the gear was fixed in the nick of time, and our captain turned calmly from his grim task, rose and retrieved the wheel from another member of the crew; then he smiled and said, pointing straight ahead, "There lies Bluefield!"

Bluefield was another small island that we had to pass on the way home. The captain wished to stop there to visit an old friend and to give us a pause after all that excitement. I never understood, at the time, how his presence and personality made that near disaster seem so harmless, how he made us feel that no real harm could have came to us while he was there. It was long after that when I fully appreciated how close we were to a tragic ending.

The next day, after we returned to Bocas Town, he preached a most inspiring sermon in which the theme was, "God on the Bridge." He said we should let God pilot our lives even in the deepest of troubles, on the darkest of seas, and as he spoke, I could see him on the bow of his launch when he thought his life was over many years ago, when he faced his moment of truth, of spiritual transformation that led him to give his life to the church and to the ministry. I could also see Cusapin, the reeling launch, the broken gear, the treacherous channel, and the calmness and serenity on his face throughout that entire crisis, and then I knew there was no fear of death in him—only a grace that comes from God.

## The Old Sailor

He sat in the doctor's office waiting to hear the result of his examination. The examination was completed, but the doctor was conferring with two other specialists about his findings, so as to be sure. They must have come to a final decision, as he came into the office and sat down behind his desk across from his patient, Cornelius Richard Irons. Cornelius, otherwise known as Dick, looked at the doctor.

"Well, Doc, what is the verdict? Give it to me straight, and don't pull any punches. It looks bad, doesn't it?"

Dr. Curtis looked at him almost as if he didn't want to say the words, but he knew he had to tell his patient the result of the tests.

"Mr. Irons, you see, I am afraid I have to tell you that it looks very bad! You have an advanced case of cancer, and there is nothing I can do to treat it at this stage."

"Yes, Doc, but cut the long speech and tell me how much time I got left!"

"Maybe 3 months, maybe less. It could happen in two or three weeks from now."

"I see," said Mr. Irons in a reflective tone.

The doctor continued, "At your age, this type of cancer is not unusual. I am sorry, Mr. Irons!"

"Oh, that's all right, Doc, I knew I had to go some time. It's not so bad. I am seventy-five, and I've lived long enough already. But listen, Doc, there's something I want to ask you."

"Yes, what is it?"

"Please don't tell my daughter anything about this, do you hear? I want to handle it in my own way. If she asks, just tell her it's rheumatism or some old age sickness. Okay, Doc?"

"Only if you promise to tell your children yourself," said Dr. Curtis.

"Yes, yes, I'll do that. Don't you worry, Doc."

He left the doctor's office almost as if a heavy burden had been lifted from him. At least now he knew how much time he had left, and the guessing was over. How many people are walking around in this world who are going to die within days, weeks, months or a year, and they don't even know it yet? So many of them will just drop dead, or have an accident and never even think it is going to happen to them. At least he knew the most he had were three months, and he wasn't going to feel sorry for himself. He decided he wasn't going to go straight home; he was going to take a cab, get off down by the seaside and take a walk and look at the ocean.

He always did like the sea. He remembered when he was a little boy he wanted to go to sea. He wanted to be a sailor so bad, he used to watch the ships coming and going through the Panama Canal and wishing he was on one of them. There was an old sailor who used to come from the city to visit relatives in La Boca, and Dick remembered how he would talk about faraway places like Japan, China, India, Australia and countries in South America. He would describe the Pacific Islands and the Far East till Dick could see those faraway places with his eyes closed, and the old sailor would tell seamen's jokes and thrilling adventure stories as well. He used to love to hear him sing and recite verses about the sea:

No man alive can boast like me
of the greatest adventures bar none.
Riches and wealth meant nothing to me
for I loved being a sea-fearing bum!

In the fairest of weather or in hurricanes
I sailed with the meanest, the bravest and best,
with the wind in my hair and the salt in my veins
and the rhythm of the sea throbbing in my breast.

From Alaska to the Cape to the Florida Keys,
from the China Sea to the shores of Dakar,
from Japan to Australia to the Southern Seas,
from Shanghai to Borneo to Zanzibar!

So here's to my youth, to adventure and fun,
to the life that was Heaven to me.
Lord knows, I'd give a barrel of rum
If I could return to the sea!


Oh, yes, as a boy he just knew he was going to be a sailor when he grew up! He used to read books about the sea, like **Moby Dick, Captains Courageous, Robinson Crusoe,** and **Rescue at Sea,** and stories about Blackbeard and Captain Hook—as many pirate stories as he could get his hands on.

When he was a young man, he all but joined the merchant marines. He couldn't join the U.S. Navy then, because he wasn't an American citizen, but he could join the merchant marines. Yes, he came close to joining, in the same way that Carl, Wesley, Jake and many of his boyhood friends had done; but he never did! He never did because in life, the roads we take are not always the ones we want to take, but circumstances sometimes dictate our choices and cause us to make different ones than we would like. He is not bitter about what happened, no, sir, because he would probably make the same choice again, given the same circumstances.

He was one of two children. His father had died several years back, and his brother had left for the United States, so he was the only one remaining to take care of his mother who was an invalid. He couldn't abandon her, even if it meant giving up his dream. So he postponed it, hoping that maybe one day later, if things changed, he could still pursue his ambition. But again fate stepped in, and one day he met the girl of his dreams and got married. They lived in his mother's home, and together they both cared for her, and had time to raise a family as well, and as for his dream—well, that was the end of that, even though, from time to time, he kept it alive in his heart. It would never die, really.

Now, as he glanced at the waves and the ships on the ocean, he remembered his boyhood friends who went to sea. "They are probably all dead by now, anyway," he said to himself. He knew the old sailor had long passed—bless his soul for enriching his boyhood with his stories! China, Japan, Hong Kong, Borneo, Africa—the names still stuck in his head. Maybe, thanks to that old sailor, he did go to sea after all, and sailed the high seas, at least in his imagination! It would have been nice, though, to have gone to those places in real life.

He lived out his mature years in Panama raising his family, and after many years, he retired from the Canal Zone, but when his wife, Emilia, died, he came to the U.S. to live with his youngest daughter, Adriana, who lived in Brooklyn, N.Y. It was there that he went after returning from his walk along the seashore. His daughter, who looked after him, was worried that he took so long to come home from the doctor. He told her he stopped by to visit a friend for a while.

"And what about the examination?" she asked. "What did the doctor say?"

"Oh, nothing, just a little rheumatism. You know how it is when you're getting up in age."

"Don't scare me like that again, Daddy. You know I don't want anything to happen to you!"

And he went off to his room without another word.

Three weeks later, he complained of a back pain, and he knew it must be time. His daughter rushed him to the hospital, where he was admitted without delay. There was no way, now, that he could keep her from finding out the truth. She chided him a little, but he told her he didn't want to worry her, that he was hoping he could sail on a ship far away and die somewhere at sea, so nobody could see him suffer. She chided him again for talking such things that frightened her.

He was laid up in the hospital for two more weeks before the end came. When it did, all his children, who had traveled from far away, were at his bedside. He was delirious and began hallucinating.

"I am glad you all could come to see me off! You're going to have to go ashore soon, though, because my ship is getting ready to sail. We are going to Hong Kong and the Far East, and then I am going to see the sands of Borneo, Java, and Hawaii, and we're going to Taiwan and Japan! Isn't it wonderful! I am going to sea! I am going to sea at last! Do you hear the captain calling? Yes, its time to go now. Oh, the water's so lovely, and the sky—goodbye."

And with those words, the old sailor finally went to sea after all!

## The Nickel

Jim was reaching into his wallet, and a nickel fell out. The man sitting on the stool next to him reached down, picked it up and gave it back to him—but not without a comment.

"At today's inflation rate, this coin is probably worthless! I doubt there is anything you can buy for a nickel these days. Here, this must be yours—it fell from you."

Jim thanked him as he took the coin and pressed it warmly in the palm of his hand.

"Yes, I suppose you're right. You can't buy much with a nickel, I suppose." And he carefully placed the coin back in a secret compartment of his wallet.

The barmaid gave him the change for the twenty-dollar bill he had taken out of his wallet when the nickel accidentally fell. He gave her a nice tip, placed the change in his pocket and left the bar.

As he sat in his car warming up the engine before driving off, he reached into his pocket again and took out his wallet to see if the nickel was still there. He took it out and held it in his hand tenderly and pressed it to his bosom. His mind began to wander. He was no longer sitting in his car; he was far away, years away, forty-six years to be exact! He was twelve years old! (You would think that a grown man in his fifties would have left his childhood behind, but he could not!)

He was sitting on a bench on the porch of the tenement building where he lived as a boy, in the little town called La Boca, Canal Zone. She was only eleven years old herself, and her hair was short and curly. Her skin was dark and smooth, and her eyes were bright and clear like crystals that you could look into and see a marvelous amber light surrounded by a pure marble white, as the amber dilated with the change of brightness on the porch. The amber reminded him of those small shiny marbles they used to call *aggies*, but more spectacular, and she would roll her eyeballs or

147

close her eyes whenever he stared at her too long. Her face always seemed to light up, especially when she smiled—which she was always in the habit of doing for she was always very playful and happy.

Yes, she made him feel very happy, too, whenever they were together—especially on rainy days! They would sit upstairs on the second-floor porch, looking out at the trees and the rain pitter pattering on the pavement, at the people running in the street to find shelter, at the little silly boys playing outside in the rain! They would talk silly things about what they were going to be when they grew up, what kind of house they were going to live in, the places they were going to see, and things like that. He was going to be a great professor, and she was going to be a movie star! At other times, he thought of being a sailor or a preacher, but she stuck to being a movie star! Sometimes they played jacks, or pick-up-sticks, or sometimes they read stories out loud. They would play house occasionally, even though they thought they were too old for that game.

Their world was whatever they wanted it to be, and it was rich and full no matter what was happening around them. They used to talk about saving money to buy all the things they wanted. They thought a hundred dollars could buy them the world! There wasn't that much money in all the kingdoms they had read about, they said. One day she told him, "You be our banker," and she gave him a nickel as her first installment! She had gotten it from her father to buy candy, but she said she would rather save it instead.

How innocent and vulnerable children are, thinking that their perceptions of life are all there is, and never thinking about the vicissitudes and the twists of fortune, good or bad! It wasn't three weeks after that day her family moved away! And just a few days before the departure, they were together for the last time, and they were sad—very sad. In that moment, they promised they would never forget each other, and would keep their pledges.

Children, it seems, do not fully grasp the significance of that kind of parting, at least not right away, because somehow they always seem to go on and find something else to occupy their minds, and other adventures to fill their busy play days. To them, there is too much living to do to fret and pine!

But the nickel—what about the nickel! He had forgotten about the nickel! Weeks after she had moved away, he realized he still had it and had not returned it to her! He had no way now of doing that, so he kept it as a keepsake. Even though many times after that he was tempted to spend it, whenever he held it in the palm of his hand, he could not part with it!

The years went by, and for a long time he seemed to have forgotten about Celia. Yes, Celia was her name! Beautiful Celia! The Celia of his childhood!

His family, too, later moved from La Boca to the suburbs of Panama City to a town called Rio Abajo. There, he grew into a young man, graduating from high school and starting to support himself. As nature always has it, when a young man is growing up, his thoughts, his nature turn to romance, and Jim, of course, was no exception. He started dating girls, became seriously involved with a young lady he dated, got married, had a son, and later divorced—but all the time, he kept the nickel, and in the deep recesses of his mind, he kept his remembrance of Celia!

Now, in retrospect, one might think it strange if in all those years he had never tried to find Celia; but he did try! Even when he was in his teens and living in Rio Abajo, before he got married, he had made a painstaking and thorough search to find her. He even went back to his old neighborhood and made inquiries and tried to trace her whereabouts as best he could. When he finally located her parents, they told him Celia had left the Isthmus and gone to the United States to live, that he should forget about her, that they did not want him to see her ever again, and that they did

149

not think he was right for her. They refused to give him her address, and that was when he stopped making inquiries and gave up, albeit too easily, the search.

It wasn't until many years later, after his divorce, that he, too, went to the United States to live. By a strange coincidence, one day in New York City, he ran into a childhood friend who had also known Celia very well. She told him that Celia and she were good friends and in fact were together in Chicago up to three years ago. When he became excited and insisted that she give him her address and tell him how to find Celia, how to get in touch with her, his friend's face became ashen and somber.

"You mean you don't know?"

"Don't know what?" he asked.

"She used to tell me about you, how as a girl she really loved you, although her parents were not too pleased when they realized it, saying it was foolishness and that the two of you were too young and foolish! Celia said she even tried to write you several times from Chicago, but her letters always came back, address unknown! She couldn't contact you anywhere! Things might have been different if she did—a whole lot different!"

"What are you talking about, different?"

Then she told him what had happened. "Celia had married a man who went insane and had to be put away in an institution. But, being the Christian that she was, later when he seemed to be improving, she signed him out to come home with her—the biggest mistake she ever made! One day in a fit of insanity, he brutally murdered her! She never should have married him in the first place," she said, "and she wouldn't leave him out of guilt or pity or both! Poor Celia!" She started to cry, then she collected herself and asked him to forgive her behavior.

Jim reached into his pocket and felt his wallet. He took out the nickel and held it in the palm of his hand, just to get the feel of it once more, as he thought of her, as the sadness overwhelmed him and he felt heartbroken! All the years did not matter! He would have given anything, anything just to see Celia again, just once, if that were only possible!

A horn kept honking as someone called out, "Aren't you going to move! You've been sitting there long enough!" The parking attendant came over to see if he was all right. Jim came to his senses and realized that he was in the parking lot of La Détente Supper Club in Queens, N.Y. Then he told the attendant, "Oh, I am fine! I am sorry, really! I am leaving. I am fine, thank you..." and drove away into the night.

# The Ring

As he sat in the airplane above the clouds, his mind began to travel back in time. He was a little boy again, not more than ten years old, and he had just come in from the playground where he and other boys and girls of the neighborhood played softball and kick football almost every day after school. Their playing field was usually the school ground or the open spaces between the tenement houses in La Boca, C.Z. where he grew up as a child. On this particular day, it was important that he arrive home on time, for it was a special day. As he walked into the house, his mother was there to greet him.

"You're a good boy for coming home on time—now go and wash up and come to the table to eat your supper!"

He looked at her and smiled, "Yes, Mommy, but afterwards I have a surprise for you!" And he ran to the bathroom, scrubbed himself clean, and then came to the table to dinner.

There were happy faces at the table— happy, smiling faces of his father and mother, his two brothers and two sisters; and there, too, was his favorite dish—stew chicken with peas and rice, which was all the more delicious with the special flavors his mother used. After dessert was served, and everyone was more than satisfied, his mother turned to him.

"Now, Henry, what was the surprise you had for me?"

Henry ran to his room and returned with a little package, which he gave her.

Happy birthday, Mommy! I love you, Mommy!"

"Why, thank you, Henry," she said as she opened the package. Inside was a gold-plated ring with a beautiful rhinestone set on its crown. She tried it on, but it was too small to fit on her fingers.

While she was trying on the ring, Henry said, "We read a story in school today about mothers, and afterwards the teacher recited a poem called *Somebody's Mother*! I felt so glad you are my mother I wanted to buy you something, so I took the money from my savings bank and bought you this ring, but I didn't know it was the wrong size!"

"It's a beautiful gift," she said, "even if it is too small. I will always cherish it regardless, and I love you, too, Henry! You are a good boy, the best son a mother ever had!" She hugged him and kissed him, and it made him very happy.

For almost two years after that, a day never went by unless he showed some outward sign of his love. He would offer to help more than usual around the house; he would draw pictures in school of her and bring them home; he would never leave home without kissing her on both cheeks; in short, he was a model son, though he was only ten years old.

As time went by, however, he grew interested in things away from home! There was softball, movies, pals, hanging around bigger boys, camping, and seeking out new adventures. He was still affectionate, but not like before. In his teen years, as his hormones started acting up, he began to get interested in girls and parties and the usual things that teenage boys do. He had long forgotten about the ring! The only rings he thought about now were the friendship rings he gave to girls he liked.

Chores around the house were becoming a burden he would try to get out of if he could. But his mother understood such things; after all, he was a growing boy who must learn about the world and become a man. She saw that he did not want for anything—nothing but the best for her Henry, her *wash belly*!

When, as a young man, he left home to live and work in another town, she anxiously waited for the days when he would come home on weekends to take special care of him. He was her pride and joy! When he was gone, all she worried about was Henry: how was he getting along, was he eating well, was he happy? When he came home, he wasn't fat enough for her, and she took good care of that with her special home-cooked recipes.

Soon he didn't come home on weekends, but she understood, for he was a very busy man, a very important man and, she said, he would see her when he could! A few years went by, and one Friday evening Henry came home, this time to tell her he was going far away to a foreign country where he could go further in his career and achieve the things he wanted out of life. Ever understanding, she told him, "Follow your star, and be the best you can be—that's what I want for you!" So he left and went away to the land called America to follow his star!

In his third year abroad, while a senior in college, his father passed away, and he took an emergency leave to rush back to Panama for the funeral. It was a sad occasion, but a happy one, too, for his mother got to see her *washbelly* again! After a brief stay, however, he returned to the U.S. to complete his studies. During the next few years, he continued to write home often—every week in fact; then his letters became fewer and fewer, and eventually they stopped. The years just seemed to go by swiftly after that, and before you knew it, he was in his late thirties and working very hard to achieve financial success. He never went home again, and his mother never saw him again, although she thought about him and asked about him and prayed for him. He was ever on her mind, and not a day went by that she did not ask, "How is Henry doing? How is my son? Tell him I love him!"

Meanwhile Henry had become an executive in a small company, working day and night. Any thought of home he put aside. "One day," he said to himself, "I'll go home again!" But that day never came, and more years went by until what seemed like yesterday turned into thirty years since he had left home. He was always too busy! Never seemed to have time! Panama was too far away! He made up excuses, too many excuses to himself, until one day, sitting in his office quite alone and feeling sad, he thought about home, his mother and his childhood, "Surely it was just yesterday," he said to himself. "It can't be thirty years already!" And in his mind he saw himself running into his mother's arms to tell her how much he loved her, and then the guilt welled up inside. "Lord, what if I never get to see her again!" The conscience of the little boy, pushed aside so long, overwhelmed him! Nothing else mattered now; he had to see her, to see for himself how she was.

It was in early spring, about 2 p.m., when he sat at the desk in his office and decided to write a long letter to his sister and brother in Panama. They were taking care of their mother for she was getting old, and her sight was very poor. He said they could read the letter to her, and he poured out his heart to her. He closed the letter by telling them of his plans to come home for a visit later that summer, that nothing would prevent him from doing so. On his way home, he mailed the letter.

Now, by a strange coincidence, his sister had sent him a telegram at about the same time he had written his letter, and the telegram was waiting for him when he arrived home that evening. The telegram informed him that if he wanted to see his mother alive again, he had better come quickly, because she had suddenly taken seriously ill. In fact, she was dying and was asking for him, calling out his name, "Henry, tell Henry I am fine, not to worry, he mustn't worry! He is a fine boy, the best son a mother ever had!" As he read those words, he could bear it no longer; his heart broke into a thousand pieces, and he sobbed uncontrollably.

And that is how he came to be on that flight one evening in the spring of 1989 heading for Panama, thinking about the past and wondering when he stopped being a little boy. He couldn't remember! How he would have loved to turn back the clock!

Finally, about 7:30 p.m. the plane landed in Tocumen Airport, Panama City, and his brother who awaited his arrival took him straight to their mother's home in Rio Abajo as fast as they could go! All along the route, Henry kept saying, "Hurry, hurry! I hope it's not too late!"

When they arrived, they saw people standing downstairs. All they said was, "Hurry!" and moved aside to let them pass. As they ran up the stairs and entered the house, they saw people inside as well, and as Henry and his brother approached the bedroom, the people who were standing around were crying! They told him that his mother had passed away only a minute ago, and her last words were, "Henry..." He ran to her, completely out of control of his emotions, and cried like a baby, begging her to forgive him. They tried to console him, but it didn't help. Then he kissed her on both cheeks and took her hand. He noticed her left hand was clenched tight even in death. When he managed to open it, he saw in the palm of her hand the ring he had given her forty years ago, when he was a little boy! She had kept it all these years and never parted with it, even to her very last breath!

### The Black Madonna

One day a teen-age daughter was curious about a piece of jewelry around her mother's neck. She kept pestering her mother and asking to see and touch it because she was so fascinated by it. "Mommy, it is so pretty! Where did it come from?"

"Come," said her mother. "Since you are so inquisitive and wouldn't leave me be, sit down, and I will tell you a story.

Many years ago when my great grandmamma, your great, great grandmamma, passed away, there was a haggling over her meager estate. Being poor, she could hardly have left anything, but you know how poor relatives are! Since she was a very thrifty person, and known to horde pennies, it was thought by everyone that she had left some money—perhaps a secret bank account, a hidden cash box, a stash hidden in an old trunk or under a floorboard, or behind a secret wall. Anyway, all her relatives haggled and fought over the things she left behind— clothes, furniture, trinkets, and a small insurance. Among the meager things she left, along with the trinkets and the cheap artifacts, was a miniature black Madonna, for she was a very spiritual person, and the Virgin Mary was her patron saint. This black Madonna was no more than six or eight inches tall and looked quite ordinary as far as workmanship was concerned. It might even have been carved by Great Grandmamma herself. They wanted to throw it away as they did many of her things that they said were worthless trinkets and rubbish, for Great Grandmamma used to collect all kinds of trivial things. But my grandmother, being religious herself, and sentimental, implored her other relatives to allow her to keep that small item which, of course, they allowed

157

since they said it was worthless, and since my grandmother agreed to waive any claims she might have had to the other things, including the small insurance, in Great Grandmamma's estate. The matter was settled therefore.

As time went by, whenever they visited my grandmother and saw the crudely carved black statuette, they asked her, "Why you keep that ugly, old thing anyway? It doesn't even belong with the other fine brass and silver ornaments you've got. Besides, you can buy a much better statue of the Madonna in a dozen different places!"

Grandmother would only nod her head and say, "Yes, I suppose you are right!" And after awhile she removed it off the shelf, but she didn't throw it away, because she was sentimental, and because it was something material that connected her with Great Grandmamma. So she put it away in her trunk for safekeeping.

Once, when my mother was a little girl, as she later told me, she saw my grandmother rummaging through her trunk, and she spied the Madonna. She asked her, "Mama, what is that?" and Grandmother told her, "It's a little statue thing, you see!"

My mother insisted, "Why is it black!"

"It belonged to your grandmother," she replied.

"But why is it black?" the child persisted.

"I suppose it could be black just as well as any other color. No one knows what the Virgin Mary really looked like. I suppose Great Grandmamma, who it first belonged to, liked to think of the Virgin that way! Now you run along, and don't ask any more silly questions!"

Anyway, when Grandmother died, my mother, Wilhelmina, found it among Grandmother's personal things, and she kept it because she remembered Grandmother saying, "It belonged to my mother. I don't know why, but I feel closer to her as long as I keep it. I believed she wanted me to!" And my mother, too, kept it the same way, as a memento of Great Grandmamma, and as something she could point to that was handed down from generation to generation—and she kept it only for that reason, she said, although it seemed to be more than that, for there was a strange attachment to the black Madonna that she couldn't even explain. She hid it away among her personal things like her mother before her, all through the years.

Later in life when I grew up, got married and was raising you and your brother and sister, my mother, who was getting up in age and sensing that she did not have much longer to be on this earth, called me and sat me down to talk about it. "Now, dear daughter," she said, "you know I won't be with you much longer. Ever since your father passed away and left me years ago, there wasn't much reason to go on living anyhow, except for you, our only child. You know I am very poor, and I don't have much to leave you. I made a will for you to get the little insurance and whatever you see in this apartment, but there is something else I want you to have even before I pass away, for I believe it has brought me good luck and will do the same for you!" And she went inside her bedroom and came back with the little black Madonna in her hand. She held it so dearly to her bosom as if she didn't want to part with it. "It was my grandmother's," she said. "I can't explain it, but somehow I know she wanted you to have it. It will bring you good luck, I am sure!" And she gave me the black Madonna. A few months later, my mother passed away in her sleep one night.

Even though I had my own family around me, life seemed lonelier without her.

Several years went by, and life's ups and downs—more downs than ups—began to take their toll. We came upon hard times. Your father, Henry, and I were divorced, and he was late with the alimony payments; bills were piling up; you children needed new clothes and money for school; the rent payment was falling behind; and I had received a temporary lay-off notice from my job at Charles Schwab and Company. The creditors were already calling on the phone regarding the late payments, and I was depleting the little savings I had and was near desperation! I didn't know what to do! I remember I was rushing to answer the telephone one day when, accidentally, I knocked the black Madonna off the shelf where I kept it. When it fell, it received a severe dent and a scratch that were noticeable. After hanging up the phone, having told the caller (though I don't know why) they would get their payment by the end of the month, I examined the damage to the Madonna more closely. I noticed that the head was dented and twisted badly, so I took it to the Ajax appliance repair shop and asked Mr. Kamis to fix it for me while I waited. He straightened out the dented and twisted statuette, but in doing so some of the paint came off. He showed it to me and said, "It looks like underneath the black exterior is a coat of white, and beneath that the natural color of the metal has a yellowish tint. It could be some kind of copper-based metal. I could remove all of the paint if you like. In any case, you'll need to put another coat of black paint on it if you want it to be the way it was." I told him I would do that myself, that I had some black paint at home. I thanked him and left the store to return home.

When I got home, I took a file and tried to scrape some more of the black paint off. It was difficult, so I went to a paint chemist and obtained the proper chemicals to remove as much of the paint as possible. It became clear that the entire statuette was made of some kind of yellow metal, just as Mr. Kamis had said. I then took it to a friend of mine who is a jeweler, who cleaned and tested it and told me the yellow metal was gold, pure gold! In fact, he said he would have it further assayed for me and tell me its real value. I trusted him, so I left the statue with him for a few days to make the necessary evaluation. When I returned, he told me, "Whoever left you this statuette left you a very valuable gift. Not only is it pure gold, but inside the statue were imbedded three genuine, sparkling diamonds. Here, I want to show them to you!" He showed me the gold and the diamonds and added, "Altogether I'd say it's worth about $90,000. You are very lucky! Your immediate financial problems are solved!" I knew, then, what my mother meant when she said she knew that Great Grandmamma wanted me to have the Madonna, and I knew also, what she meant when she said it would bring me good luck, and it came at the right time when it was truly needed. I said to myself, "Thank you, Great Grandmamma. All the way from the great beyond, you have sent this blessing to me! I thank you ever so much!"

"Well, there you have it now! How did you like the story?" said the mother.

"I liked it very much," said the daughter, "but Mama, how did you get the medallion on your neck chain?"

"That? Oh yes, I almost forgot. You see, before I left the jeweler's store, arrangements were made for the sale of the gold and diamonds, except that I had him take a small amount of the gold and make it into a little medallion, this one that you were so curious about, in the shape of the Madonna, which I have never parted with since then. It is not a black Madonna, but it came from the black Madonna handed down to me from my great grandmamma. It is pure gold, and someday I am going to give it to you as a remembrance of me, and as a remembrance of where it came from."

## Cousin Vera

In 1957, Henry came from Panama to live with his sister Helen and her husband, Bertran Martin at 25 Irving Place, Brooklyn, N.Y. They lived in a three-family house where the landlord occupied the first floor, Helen and Bertran Martin the second floor, and a younger couple occupied the third floor above them. The apartment was a two-bedroom apartment in a wood-framed house that must have been a few hundred years old. Henry had just migrated to the U. S. from Panama and had great expectations; however, this story is not about Henry or his sister; it is about Vera, his cousin!

About a year after Henry moved in with his sister, his cousin Vera, who also migrated from the Caribbean, came to stay there until she could find a place of her own. She was given Henry's room and he had to sleep in the living room on the convertible sofa-bed. At that time, Henry was going to school at night and working as a clerk in the day somewhere in Woodside, Long Island for a German import/export company. He had heard of his cousin, but this was the first time he ever met her. She was simple in appearance, gentle by nature, calm, very humble and soft-spoken with a kind of personality that seemed to quiet you in her presence. She said, "Hello, Henry, I am so pleased to meet you!" in a soft but pleasant voice and with a warm smile. He estimated at the time that cousin Vera must have been about fifty-five. She had one suitcase and a little bag, both of which contained all of her worldly possessions!

Vera was not a worldly person, as he came to know, and that was by choice, not by circumstance. Instinctively, he knew that if she was going to find happiness, it was not going to be via this world's standards, and it was not going to be in a spousal relationship, either! He, who was filled with great expectations of worldly pleasures, of meeting women and perhaps getting married, and

163

of becoming wealthy, could not understand that! He was fascinated anyway by her calm, peaceful demeanor and her celibate nature.

Each morning, Vera was up early reading her Bible and praying, and it wasn't long before Henry realized that she was very religious; in fact, religion was her whole life, as he would discover. She would offer to prepare breakfast for the family, and she could cook as good as the best. Breakfast would be ready by the time everybody had showered and dressed, so that they were always assured of being on time for work. She had a way of preparing plain and Spanish omelets that made it come out neat and appetizing! She taught Henry to make omelets, because until then he always made a mess of the eggs and could never get it to come out neat. So thanks to her, he became an expert at omelet making!

As time went by, Henry continued to have an obsession about his cousin Vera. He wondered why she had never married and never had children. It seemed that the part of her heart that was responsible for physical love for the opposite sex—if there was such a thing—was dead and gone forever!

She loved people, but in a different way! She was always most unselfish, compassionate, and kind to everyone; but her heart was dead to sensual love. Henry used to tease her and ask her why she didn't date men, or go to parties, or wear sexy clothes, and she would only say, "That's not for me. I am happy the way I am. I have given my heart, body and soul to the Lord!"

"Well," Henry thought to himself, "I do believe that the Lord wants us to make and have a family, too!" He couldn't accept her way entirely, and his obsession was not satisfied.

Finally the day came when cousin Vera found a place and was leaving the apartment. It happened that she got a position with the Christian Mission Church a block away, and she was to live upstairs above the church in her own apartment. She would be as close to the church physically as you can get. Spiritually, she became a church sister and a lay preacher, too, and went on retreats and trips, etc. She lived and breathed for God!

Henry saw her after that, but not as often as before. One Saturday morning, he visited her at the church. She was interested in how he was doing and if he was happy. She fixed him a snack and some lemonade, and they chatted. In the back of his mind, he wanted to bring up the subject of her celibacy again, but he couldn't; she seemed so contented and at peace with herself! Besides, some of her peace of mind was rubbing off on him, too. It was a pleasant visit.

Back at the apartment, since Vera moved out, his sister gave him back his room, which he reorganized and redecorated to match his personality. About a week after visiting Vera, he was cleaning up his room and changing the bed sheets. While he was rearranging the bed, he happened to rotate the mattress 180 degrees because it was sagging on one side. In the process of moving the mattress, he noticed underneath it a small black book. He couldn't imagine what it was doing there and who could have placed it there. Out of curiosity, he opened the book. Inside he found an old photograph of cousin Vera when she was very young, not more than nineteen or twenty years old! She was very pretty! On the back of the photo, it said, "I love you, Joe," in Vera's handwriting and, "I am yours forever, Vera!" There was another photograph with her posing with a handsome man much older than she was, perhaps in his thirties. They made a handsome couple. She appeared to be in love and very happy. Further in the book was a letter dated May 13, 1932. That was thirty-five years ago! He opened the letter and read its contents:

Dear Vera:

It hurts me to write this letter to you like this. I hope you do not hate me for it. I know I promised to marry you and make you my wife; but that cannot be since I have a

165

wife and family of my own. I am sorry if I led you to believe otherwise. I am returning the photographs we took. Please forgive me!

Goodbye,

Joe

Somewhere on the bottom of the letter was the impression of a teardrop that had apparently dried and left a slight smear. Reading the letter filled Henry with sadness to think of how Vera must have felt when she was nineteen and read it for the first time. Now he understood the part of cousin Vera that shut out the world of flesh, that said, no more will deception pierce this flesh, no more will this heart be broken! He understood better, then, why she never married, and never wanted to; why she turned to the only life she cared about, a life in the church. As he closed the book, he said to himself, "God bless you, cousin Vera! I hope you will be happy in the life you have chosen, because God never hurt no one!"

## The Little Black Box

Mr. and Mrs. Whittling rented apartment 6F at 87-01 Midland Parkway, Jamaica Estates, Queens, N.Y., a building which had gone co-op many years ago but began renting some units, especially since the real estate market went sour a few years back. They had been living there only three months, and although the rent was a bit high, $750, it was conveniently located near the subway, and it was a halfway decent neighborhood. Mrs. Whittling was forty-four years old, Mr. Whittling fifty. They had one son together, and Mrs. Whittling had a daughter by a former marriage. The boy was nineteen and the girl twenty-six, but neither lived with them, though they visited occasionally. Mr. Whittling worked as a construction worker for the city of New York.

Next door to the Whittlings, in apartment 6E, lived Mrs. Digman, fifty-five years old. She lived alone, though she was married. Her husband had left her twenty-five years ago, and never returned. Unfortunately, she was never blessed with children.

Mrs. Digman was the type of person who was always poking her nose into everybody's business and was given to excessive gossip about her neighbors and people in general, always complaining about something or other, even when there was nothing to complain about. She did not have many friends, and even the ones she had associated with her reluctantly. She never seemed to be happy, except when spreading some juicy piece of gossip about someone. God knows, she must not have been this way at one time, but life sours some people, and they become unhappy and meddlesome and malicious like Mrs. Digman. Most of the neighbors were really afraid to confide anything in her because as soon as they did that, the whole world would know about it. So they pretended to be her friend and usually lied to her or said very little.

It happened that, ever since the new neighbors moved next door three month ago, Mrs. Digman had been trying to find out something about them to gossip about. She watched to see when they left and when they came home, who came to visit, what type of clothes they wore, whom they talked to. She even checked the garbage containers to see if she could learn anything about them, including the kind of food they ate, the kinds of things they read, and any letters or discarded mail.

About two or three weeks later, in her eagerness and determination to learn about the Whittlings, she started listening through the wall, which was thin as paper, to learn Mrs. Whittling's secrets and personal business. She listened to conversations between Mr. and Mrs. Whittling; she even listened to conversations on the telephone. (The telephone was near the wall.) If it were possible for her to wiretap their phone, she would have done so.

One day she overheard a heated conversation between them, in which Mrs. Whittling called her husband a good-for-nothing drunkard and a slob, and he in turn called her a bastard and a prude. Well, it didn't take long before the whole neighborhood knew about that!

Then there was the time she heard Mr. Whittling say that Mrs. Whittling's daughter by a previous marriage was not good because she was pregnant and not married, and she didn't even know who the father was! And another time, she heard his wife refer to him during an argument as an *ex-jailbird*, before she met him! These pieces of news never failed to hit Mrs. Digman's gossip circuit.

One day she was listening when Mrs. Whittling received a telephone call, and she heard Mrs. Whittling laughing and carrying on, saying to the person on the other end, "Honey, you know how I feel. I want to just as much as you! Maybe we can meet on Friday!" And with that, the word got out that Mrs. Whittling had a secret lover!

By now, the gossip was catching up to the Whittlings, because whenever Mrs. Whittling went to the laundry room, her neighbors looked at her suspiciously and started whispering behind her back. Sometimes they put little notes under her door like, "Jailbird!" or "Bastard!" or "Stop trying to be uppity, you are no better than the rest of us, you and your jailbird husband can go to blankety!"

Life was getting to be hell for them, and although at first they did not know who was behind it, they soon realized that there was only one way people could know these things, since they said them within the privacy of their apartment. So they decided on a plan to prove their theory.

The following is a conversation that ensued as part of their plan. Of course, Mrs. Digman was listening on the other side.

"Harry, what are we going to do with all that money? You know it isn't ours, and if those people find out, what will happen to us? You know they are coming here tomorrow and if they find it here in the apartment, we will be in an awful lot of trouble! At least if we got rid of it for a while, they couldn't find it here, and they might leave us alone! Then tomorrow night we could get it back and figure out then what to do with it!"

"Yes, Mary, but what are we going to do with it? Where are we going to hide it?"

"I know what we'll do. You see that little black box that the USPE item came in two days ago? Put the money in it and bury it!"

"But where are we going to bury it?"

"In the back yard, stupid! Wait until everybody is asleep tonight, around 2 a.m., and go out back and bury it in the little black box. Mark the spot, then we will wait until tomorrow night!"

"That's a very good idea, honey—I'll do it tonight!"

Now, in the meantime, Mrs. Digman had her ears glued to the wall and heard the whole conversation. She decided she was going to sneak out before him at 1:45 a.m. and hide in the landry room. Then as he passed by, she would watch where he buried the money, and after he left she would dig it up, and all that money would be hers! At least that's what she thought!

So everything was set! At exactly 1:45 a.m., Mrs. Digman went down to the laundry room and waited. At 2:00 a.m. sharp, Mr. Whittling left his apartment with the black box under one arm and a small shovel in the other. He headed straight for the back of the house and found him a good spot by a clump of bushes, where he buried the box and marked it carefully by placing three stones around it, each stone one foot from the center of a triangle, with the center the spot where the box was buried. He was satisfied. All they had to do now was to wait!

He headed straight back to his apartment to tell his wife that all had gone well. Mrs. Digman made sure he had gone back upstairs and twenty minutes later went out back and dug up the little black box, put it in a shopping bag she took with her, and returned to her apartment with her stolen treasure. The Whittlings, meanwhile, were awake, and they, in turn, sat quietly in their apartment waiting!

At exactly 3:00 a.m., a horrible scream was heard coming from apartment 6E. It was so loud and frightening, it woke the entire building out of their sleep! Everyone wondered what had happened and if some terrible crime had been committed. Several people including the super rushed to apartment 6E to see what had happened. They banged on the door, and then the super used his master key and opened the door. To their amazement and horror, they saw Mrs. Digman standing petrified, white as a sheet, motionless and speechless! Then they saw the little black box on the floor. A three-foot snake had crawled out of it and was trying to find some place to hide. It must have been scared, itself, by Mrs. Digman's screaming!

Well, the fact that it was a non-poisonous snake didn't matter; it served its purpose quite well. As for Mrs. Digman, she never regained her speech, and is still going to a therapist to this day! If she ever talks again, it is certain she will never gossip or poke her nose into other people's business anymore.

# Fighting Fire with Fire

The Midland Gardens is a seven-story apartment building, just like Wexford Terrace, in Jamaica Estates, Queens, that had also gone co-op many years ago. When in the eighties the real estate market skyrocketed, and co-ops weren't selling as well as before, some units were rented out under one- and two-year leases with options to buy. Number 6F was one such apartment.

In apartment 7F lived an old lady, Mrs. Olewitch, who, along with her husband, had fought the landlord when he was converting the apartment building years ago to co-op, and, using some mysterious influence, they were able to keep living as the only renting tenants at the time of conversion, paying their same old rent besides. The landlord, it seemed, was afraid to tangle with Mrs. Olewitch and made a special accommodation for her. It was also true that in the building many residents were afraid to cross paths with Mrs. Olewitch, for, like her sister who lived in the Wexford Terrace apartment building a block away, she had become a problem for her neighbors as well as the landlord. They could do nothing with her.

She was always acting suspiciously and had a way that caused you to believe there was a sinister motive for everything she did or said. Although she was small of stature and frail in appearance, it was misleading and was one of her weapons to catch you off-guard. You were more likely to be her victim than she yours. She was vindictive, malicious, devious, scheming—in short, dangerous. In fact, she was a witch!

Her face was dried up, and if you looked closely you saw that she had a few carbuncles, bloodshot eyes, and yellow teeth. (One or two were missing!) Her facial expression was constricted from years of frowning, ill will and evildoing, so that if she smiled, it was at the risk of the facial tissues breaking up! Her skin was pale and jaundiced, and when she spoke it was like a person speaking who

172

could barely open her mouth. So tight and strictured it was (it might even have been a neuromuscular malady of some kind), that it caused her to speak with a grating, irritating sound.

When Henry Mitchell, a city clerk, moved into apartment 6F, below Mrs. Olewitch, little did he know what he was in for. The first three weeks of grace, things were fine indeed. He didn't even know who she was at that time. But that didn't last long. He soon started seeing notes Scotch-taped onto his door, then letters were slipped under the door as well. This was her way of introducing herself to him, to let him know, it appears, who ran the building and how he must behave in his apartment if he wanted to continue living there. The notes insinuated that he couldn't play his radio or hi-fi, nor TV after certain hours, nor above a certain volume anytime. He certainly couldn't play his piano at any time at all, day or night, according to her rules, for she hated music and all musicians as well. Once, she came down to his door ostensibly to complain, but perhaps more accurately to see what was in his apartment or who else was living there. (She was a busy-body, too, of course!) She tried to intimidate him or test him out, warning him that she would take stern measures if she thought he would give her any trouble.

Henry completely ignored her and turned her away from his door. He was sorely annoyed by her, her notes and her harassment. She didn't like the idea of his living there either, for whatever reason, so she stepped up her campaign to remove him! After the notes came the rotten eggs and garbage left outside his door. When that didn't work, it appeared she recruited a sister witch below him in apartment 5F to join the campaign. They must have successfully joined forces before, for their alliance was formidable. They were both very busy night and day, trying to achieve their objective of forcing him to leave. Henry did everything he could for peace, even taking off his shoes whenever he entered the apartment, because they said he walked too hard. (He only weighed 150 lbs and wore rubber heels and slippers.) He bought extra rugs, covering the piano with a heavy rug and playing only between 5:00 and 7:00 p.m. a few times a week, and sometimes a couple hours on the weekend, but that wasn't good enough, so he stopped playing altogether. But they insisted they could still hear every movement he made in his apartment, even when he turned over in his bed, or got out of bed late at night to go to the bathroom, and that was disturbing because it woke them up. Even when he breathed and yawned, they could tell.

They continued this attack for some time, and when that didn't work, he started hearing strange sounds coming from upstairs, like someone stomping and pacing the floor above him, chanting and uttering strange animal sounds. The old-timers from the Caribbean, where Henry was born, would say it sounded like a ritual of some kind (obeah, in other words!). The sound and chanting would go on for hours at a time, and it was spooking the apartment somewhat, spooking Henry, too, as a matter of fact.

One evening when he was coming home from work, a young lady, a Latina, stopped him on the street and asked, "Are you the new tenant in 6F, Midland Gardens?"

"Yes, as a matter of fact. Why?"

"Oh, my name is Maria Prieto. You see, I used to live in that same apartment before you moved in, but I had to move out. Thank God I did! I now live a couple blocks away! I couldn't take it any longer—they hounded me and put me through hell! I am glad I left!"

Henry started to say, "What…" but she interrupted.

"That witch above you, Mrs. What's her name, she started writing you notes yet?"

"Yes," said Henry.

"She started stomping and chanting and putting garbage outside your door?"

174

Henry began to feel that it wasn't he that was the problem after all, since someone else had the identical experience he was having. Maria continued.

"I got out of there before she cast some evil spell on me. You better watch out, I am telling you!"

Her remarks didn't do any good for Henry's peace of mind. Not that he really believed in witchcraft or such, but you must admit, being around certain negative and evil people can be disquieting.

In the days and weeks that followed, some of the things Maria said were confirmed by the super and several other tenants in the building. Their remark, almost without exception, was, "Is that sick lady at it again?" for they had apparently either had some unpleasant experience with her or knew others who did. They empathized with Henry, and though their empathy helped a little, it did not remove his fears and continued annoyance. The person who was the source of his annoyance had even written a letter to the landlord telling him lies, that Henry was some kind of criminal who brought drugs in the building, disturbed the peace, and was a threat to her and other tenants, and she wanted something done about it. Of course, the only other tenant she could be referring to was her cohort, or sister witch in 5F, Ms. Bell, who, as was stated, was already part of her conspiracy. The landlord did not take her seriously because he knew her reputation, though he did warn Henry Mitchell that he was her target and he should try to ignore her and watch his back!

Things started happening to Henry, like his car windshield being smashed twice within the same week, his mail being tampered with, strange threatening telephone calls coming in, and the mess behind his door. He was able to deal with those kinds of harassment, but obeah was another matter. He suspected that Mrs. Olewitch and Ms. Bell were getting together in each other's apartment and practicing witchcraft or some kind of voodoo rituals.

It must have been having its effect, because he would waken suddenly in the wee hours of morning with cold sweat all over his body, shaking with fright, and hearing all kinds of strange voices and sounds like someone, or something, was calling out his name and telling him to leave the apartment. There were more than one voice sometimes, and they would alternate or would be heard in a chorus. "L-e-e-e-e-v-v-v-e....! L-e-e-e-e-v-v-e! before ...something... terrible... happens ...to you! We...want...you.to...l--e-e-v-v-e!" The poor man couldn't sleep at night, so he decided to fight fire with fire!

He made inquiries among his friends in the Caribbean community and was referred to someone versed in the art of making counter spells to fight off evil spirits! He was put in touch with one Miss Sarah, as she was called, who was a famous spiritualist (obeah woman in some circles) and got her to come to his apartment and work a powerful spell that would reverse what was going on.

Well, Ms. Sarah came all the way from the island, and if the people upstairs didn't know who they were dealing with, they would soon find out. She brought her paraphernalia of witch's brew, incense, goat's dung, witch hazel, monkey paws, witch's dust, and candles into Henry's apartment one evening to do battle. She set up her stuff, and while they were raising hell upstairs, she began her own counter spell. It was something to behold! Candles were lit in the center of the room, incense was burning, she had a shaker in her hand made from some kind of dried leaves, and she began to speak a strange tongue. Her whole body started to shake violently, then she went into a voodoo chant while rhythmically stomping around the room, scattering obeah dust, rattling the leaves, huffing and puffing, dipping her head down, then raising it up to the ceiling. At one point her chant sounded like she was saying, "Hummm, hummm, hummm, hummm, go back... to the one..you came from. Hummm, hummm, hummm, humm, go back...to the one...you came from," over and over. She chanted in the living room, in the bedroom, in the kitchen, all over the apartment, and it is certain they heard her upstairs.

Something was taking its effect already because at one point, strange screams and gasps were heard coming from upstairs when their chanting suddenly stopped, and only Sarah's could be heard. Sarah's seemed to get stronger and stronger, and she suddenly stopped and raised both hands toward the ceiling and gave a hideous cry like a curse. The floor above rattled, the room shook, and then there was complete silence. A wonderful, positive energy filled the room, a wholesome, peaceful atmosphere prevailed, and she turned to Henry after a few minutes, shook the leaves over his head and all around his body, hugged him and said, "You will have no more trouble from them again!"

Before she left his apartment, she gave him some extra candles, incense, and an amulet she said would protect him anywhere he went, because you didn't know when or where evil spirits might attack.

Whether you believe in witchcraft or not, from that night on Henry slept like a log, and he never saw or heard anymore from Mrs. Olewitch or Ms. Bell. After several weeks, he got to wondering, especially when he saw a huge moving van downstairs, and he inquired of the super.

"Ms. Bell is moving out," said the super, "and you know, Mrs. Olewitch is in a sanitarium. She went berserk! I don't think we will be seeing her around here anymore!"

A week later the landlord called him and asked him if he knew anyone who needed an apartment; he had a vacancy in 5F. "By the way," he said, "are things any better with you lately?"

Henry said, "Yes, a lot, thank you!

But of course the landlord knew what had happened, and no one was happier than he was because he couldn't get rid of the witch. It took Sarah, the *baddest* obeah woman in town, to do it.

## Russian Roulette

On Wednesday nights, business was a little slow in Harry's bar. Usually when there was a slow night, Ceci, the bar mistress, didn't mind the guys telling stories, or playing a little poker in the back room or messing with the game machine. In fact she would join them herself, sometimes, to kill the time, and she was fun-loving by nature. You never met a woman more fun-loving, more uninhibited, loose-tongued and crazy! She would do and say the craziest things, it's a good thing no church-going, righteous people were around to hear her sinning the way she did! She would swear up and down the alphabet, with more four-letter words than you can imagine; and it wouldn't be past her to expose herself, if that would bring a wave of excitement! Actually her body parts were always overexposed anyway, so a newer revelation by her never caused too much stir. Whenever the guys told yarns, she always had a bigger one so as not to be outdone. On Wednesday nights, therefore, it wasn't unusual to see her and her regulars tossing coins to see who could match heads or tails, throwing darts, even throwing dice from a cup onto the bar, arm wrestling, or whatever diversion they thought up whereby they could wager on the outcome. They used to test each other out by doing little tricks like staring at each other to see who would blink first, while a match or lighted cigarette lighter was held between their faces; holding each other's breath to see who could hold out longest; holding a bottle of liquor to their heads to see who could gobble it down straight in one gulp without stopping!

Ceci never took a back seat to anyone—man, woman or beast! She had nerves like steel and wasn't scared of anything. Anybody dared her, she would take them up on it. "Fearless Ceci", they would call her, and she had the size to back her up at that! She weighed close to two hundred pounds with large biceps for a woman. In spite of her size, she was pleasing to look at and had a nice-looking face. Anyway, the regulars loved to hang out there because with her, something exciting was always happening.

That brings us to the Wednesday night in May of 1984, when Big Red walked into Harry's bar. Big Red was the kind of person who was always loaded, but he never had a job. He never worked a day in his life for an honest living, but he drove big cars and dressed really sharp, and he loved to gamble! He remembered the last time he was in Harry's, Ceci had beaten him out of $200 and he wasn't too pleased about that! He sat down at the far end of the bar counter and asked for his usual, bourbon and water!

"Hi, Big Red," said Ceci as she poured the bourbon, "how's tricks?"

"Everything's cool," responded Big Red. "How's everything with you, big mamma?"

"Everything is fine, just killing some time with the fellows on a slow night, you know what I mean!" Before she finished talking to Big Red, one of the guys called out to her to come and finish the game of coin flipping 'cause they had a bet going. She reacted, "I am taking care of my customer. Besides, you guys have to think of something new. Coin flipping is too tame for my blood! Ain't that right, Big Red?"

Big Red didn't say anything, but slowly reached into his coat and took out a .38 revolver and laid it on the counter. Everyone in the bar became quiet, eyes wide open looking at the revolver! Ceci spoke. "You ain't thinking of holding up the place, are you B.R.?"

"No, nothing like that! You said you wanted excitement!"

"Yeah, I ain't scared of nothing! Little piece of .38 don't frighten me! What you got in mind, B.R.?" Big Red picked up the gun and pointed it straight at Ceci! Everybody else in the bar ducked down below the counter or took cover under a table, but Ceci just stood there, 'cause she could bluff, and she was sure he wasn't going to pull the trigger. She was right; he was just testing her.

"You got a lot of nerve all right, woman!" He turned the gun away and started to empty out the bullets from the chambers, except for one bullet. Then he spun the barrel around a few times and set the gun back on the counter in front of Ceci. "I got a new game for you! Ever heard of Russian Roulette?"

"Yeah, I heard about it—what you want, to play Russian Roulette?"

"Maybe!"

"Well, I'm game if you are! I bet you the $200 I won from you I can beat you at that game, too! Is it a bet?"

Big Red nodded his head. "Its a deal," he said.

Ceci picked up the revolver, spun the barrel, and pointed it at Big Red menacingly. "Should I pull the trigger, B.R.?"

"No", said Big Red, "that's not how the game is played!"

But Ceci knew, so she turned the revolver, pointed it to her head and pulled the trigger before anyone could wink. Click. An empty chamber! A sigh of relief went across the room as she handed the gun to Big Red. "Your turn, brother man!" Big Red looked at her and looked around the room. Then he looked at the revolver and slowly held it in his hand. He pointed it to his head, and again the room became deathly quiet, with all eyes transfixed onto him. He hesitated a few seconds; then he pulled the trigger, and again the hammer struck an empty chamber. Click! B.R. and everyone in the room breathed a sigh of relief.

B.R. wiped the perspiration off his forehead and said to Ceci, "Blow your head off, sister—it's your turn!"

Ceci still showed no sign of cracking, even though the tension in that room by then was excruciating! It was her turn, and she wasn't going to back down, no sir! She spun the barrel, then pointed the revolver at her brain, and, as if she

180

didn't want to prolong the agony and suspense, pulled the trigger without hesitating. Click! Again nothing happened!

Meanwhile Big Red was squirming as in his own mind he started to wonder if it was worth it to risk his life for $200. How many times could he do this before his luck ran out? Maybe he should let that crazy woman win! But if he did that, the whole purpose for which he came there would be defeated, and he would lose face! He picked up the gun and spun the barrel, perspiration flowing down his neck and forehead as he held the nozzle to his temple. His hand began to tremble a little, then the hesitation, then tenseness, then silence as he squeezed in full view of everyone. Click! You could see the utter relief that came over him as his body relaxed. He laid the gun on the counter once more, for Ceci, and said, "It's all yours, baby!"

"Thanks for nothing," said Ceci as she picked up the revolver, wondering where that single bullet was. Was it in the next chamber, she wondered after she spun the barrel. Was it waiting for her this time, or could she draw a blank once more? For the first time, Fearless Ceci felt a little uneasy. Were her nerves finally giving out on her? Was this her last trick? She spun the gun barrel. She hesitated, then she held the revolver to her temple.

Everyone in the room became still, many of them with fingers crossed, fear and tenseness gripping them as they witnessed this death-defying spectacle by two maniacs! One more instant and brains would go flying across the room, or death would be cheated one more time. Which would it be?

Ceci looked in the mirror, then she looked at Big Red, then, calmly, she pointed the gun at her temple and pulled the trigger. Bang! The gun went off; it was not blank this time! Oh no, this time it was for real! The explosion filled the room, and the loud echo resounded. Bang! But Ceci was still standing; her brain cells were still intact! At the very last second, a sixth sense made her aim the gun at the mirror, shattering it into a thousand pieces! Better that than her brains, she thought! Then she walked over to Big Red and said, "I think my life is worth more than 200 lousy bucks. Here's your g.d. 200 bucks! Now we're even, Big Red!"

## M.E. Phistopheles

Eight days before Christmas, and Chris was desperate because he could not face his wife and children to tell them he had just lost his job, and there would be no money for Christmas presents— not even enough to pay the rent which was months in arrears, and no money to put food on the table, even on Christmas day. He was already over his head in debts, was behind in the payments, was barely squeaking by, and now, with all that, no job besides. He could not face up to telling them the truth. When he came home that evening, there was no way he was going to tell them, at least not right away, not until he had had a chance to think it out and figure out how he was going to manage. So he came home as if nothing had happened and told his wife he was tired and would lie down awhile before supper. As he lay in bed, his mind was feverishly working. What was he going to do? How was he going to pay the rent, feed his family, pay his debts? He needed more time, he thought, as his wife Mary called him to come and eat supper. At the dinner table, as he watched the faces of his three children and his wife, knowing the holiday was all the children were thinking of, he felt sad and defeated inside, but he pretended otherwise as he listened to them talk about their Christmas wish list. That night he went to bed terribly sad and broken in spirit, though he kept his feelings to himself.

The next day he left home as if he was going to work as usual, as if by doing that the problem would disappear, or some miracle would happen, and he would either get his job back or find another before he ran out of options or out of time. He spent the first day trying to find a job by calling on all the CEOs and personnel managers in all the companies he knew while he worked for I.B.M., but with no success. They were laying off workers, too, and were afraid for their own jobs. Things looked really bad!

Three more days went by. It was now Friday evening, four days before Christmas, and he knew he could not come home that evening and pretend any longer. He called home around 5:30 p.m. and told his wife he would be coming home late, not to wait up for him, he had overtime work at the company. Instead of going home, he hit all the dives and bars, trying to bury his troubles and frustrations. He ended up in a dive somewhere on the lower east side of New York City.

He was sitting on a bar stool at the end of the bar, drowning his sorrows, when he observed a gentleman with a goatee, long moustache pointed at the ends, thick eyebrows and sharp, beady eyes, sitting alone at a table in a corner of the bar. The man called the waiter over and told him something. Shortly afterwards, the bartender gave Chris a complimentary drink and said it was from the gentleman sitting at the far table. Chris took the drink and looked over at the table to thank his benefactor. The gentleman smiled and made a sign for Chris to join him. Chris accepted the invitation, and as he sat down they introduced themselves to each other. The strange gentleman spoke first. "My name is Dr. M. E. Phistopheles, at your service!"

Chris started to say, "And mine is..." but Dr. Phistopheles finished it for him.

"Christopher Springer, correct?"

"Yes, but how did you know?"

"That does not matter, really. What does matter is that I have the solution to all your troubles!"

"What do you mean?" replied Chris.

Dr. P. continued, "I know all about your situation, but how I know is not important. What would you give me, in return, if I could make you a rich man by Wednesday night, around this time, so that you would not have to work for anyone again, and you could buy your family all the things they wanted, pay off all your debts, and never have to worry about money again?"

"You're crazy," answered Chris, half wanting to believe and disbelieve at the same time.

184

"I am far from crazy! But you didn't answer my question!" said Dr. P.

"Just for argument's sake," said Chris, "if you could do what you said, I would give you anything, anything in this world, but I doubt you could do it!"

"In any case, in your predicament, what have you got to lose?" said Dr. P.

"I said I would give you anything, didn't I?" retorted Chris.

"Well", said Dr. Phistopheles, "would you give an arm?"

"Yes!"

"Would you give a leg?"

"Anything that would save my family from poverty!"

"Then would you give your soul?" said Dr. Phistopheles with such seriousness that Chris believed he meant every word of it.

Chris pondered a second then said, "If I said I would give you anything, that's what I meant!"

"Good," said Dr. P. "I propose we go to my office a block away from here and finalize the details of our agreement."

They left the bar together about 10:00 p.m. and walked a few blocks to an abandoned building to which, it seemed, Dr. Phistopheles had a key or some way of getting in, because they had no trouble entering. Somehow, in that abandoned building, there was an office with a desk, and Dr. P. lit a lamp and sat behind the desk, then pulled out a partially completed written agreement which said that he, Chris Springer, was agreeing to give up, for the sum of eighteen million dollars, his immortal soul on the blank day of blank...etc. They haggled over the missing date, and Dr. P. conceded latitude in time and allowed four months, but no later than Easter Sunday of the next year. The agreement then read, "Whereas I, Christopher Springer, of sound mind and body, do agree to relinquish to one Dr. M. E. Phistopheles, for the sum of eighteen millions dollars, my immortal soul at exactly midnight on the third Sunday of April of the coming year, this agreement becomes binding upon my signing the same."

But before Chris signed, he made him include a clause that the contract would be null and void if either party did not stick to the agreed terms to the letter. Dr. P. said he was a gentleman about such things and agreed to those terms. Then Chris said, "There is one more thing—how will I receive the payment?"

Dr. Phistopheles took out a piece of paper from his pocket and said, "On this piece of paper are written the six numbers that will play in the N.Y.S. lottery five days from today, Wednesday, the twenty-sixth. All you have to do is purchase the ticket with these numbers, and you will be the sole winner; if not, you are under no obligation to keep the agreement we made." He made sure, however, that he did not give Chris the numbers until after he had signed, and he, Dr. Phistopheles, had countersigned.

Then Chris left the building, but as he was leaving, he could hear behind him a weird, diabolical laugh echoing from the building. He hurried to the subway and went home to Queens, N.Y. to his family. He felt uneasy about the whole thing and for a while wasn't quite convinced that it had really taken place. He knew he was not too drunk, but what really convinced him was the fact that in his pocket he had the six numbers!

On Monday morning, he bought the six numbers, and, on the strength of it, decided to spend whatever credit he still had as well as the balance of the unpaid rent money they were saving, although it was already overdue. He bought a few presents and a fat capon for Christmas dinner!

Tuesday Christmas arrived, even though dubiously, to the Springers' apartment. They had a wonderful Christmas dinner, gifts for the children and all, and the following night, Wednesday night, Chris sat glued to the TV set as, lo and behold, the six numbers came out just as Dr. Phistopheles had said they would. Chris was a millionaire! They were so happy that most of the night they stayed up celebrating and finally retired after 2 a.m.

Needless to say, their lifestyle was drastically changed after that! They paid off all their debts, bought a home in the suburbs, a brand new car, new furniture, and clothes, and took a vacation in late January. They even shared some of their wealth with relatives and friends. They were the happiest family!

By now, Chris had forgotten all about the agreement; however, February, March and April came around very quickly. It was now April twenty-fifth, and he realized that within twenty-four hours, there would be a reckoning for his sudden good fortune. His wife observed his changed mood and tried to find out why a man who had everything he wanted in the world was pacing the house like a man with troubles. That is when he confided to her, "Mary, all this good fortune didn't happen by chance. There's more to it that you don't know about! I tried to keep it from you just like I did about my losing my job, but now I don't know!"

"Don't know what, Chris? You didn't keep anything from me as you say. I had known about your layoff, but I didn't say anything because I knew sooner or later you would have told me. I just thought it was a God-sent blessing when we won the lottery! What, then, is this thing you don't know how to tell me?"

And he confided in her the whole story of how he met Dr. M. E. Phistopheles that night in December, and they had signed the contract. She asked him to show her his copy of the contract, and she read it through carefully, then said, "I want to be by your side tomorrow night when this Dr. Phistopheles comes, if he dares to come here!"

The next night, Sunday, April twenty-sixth, Chris and Mary sat up in their living room waiting, while the children were all in bed sleeping. It was very late, and Mary tried to console Chris by telling him not to worry. They would face it together; in any case, he might not even show up! As she said that, Dr. Phistopheles appeared before them in the living room, looking most satisfied with himself. He said,"You know, Christopher, I was most generous with you—I get most of my clients much cheaper! Yes, sir, it is midnight, and as we agreed, I am here to collect. Shall we be going?"

Just then, Mary jumped in between them and said to Dr. Phistopheles, "Going where—where you going with my husband? Look here now, you Mr. Phesto or Topless or whatever your name is, what business you got with my husband?"

"Why, Mrs. Springer, I am afraid you don't understand, but I'm sure your husband must have explained everything to you about our contract! You know, a bargain is a bargain is a bargain, and I always keep my part! So must your husband!"

"Well now, hold it one moment there now, what business you got coming into our house at one o'clock Monday morning? I read your so-called agreement—it said nothing about one o'clock!"

M. E. Phistopheles' face started to get redder and redder as he saw that this wasn't going to be easy at all. He replied, "What's this about one o'clock; it's midnight, midnight, midnight! You can't cheat me—it's midnight!"

"Oh, no you don't, not so fast," said Mary. "You never heard 'bout Daylight Savings Time? I see you not so smart as you think you are. It's way past midnight—you're one hour late, in fact. It is now 1 a.m., April twenty-seventh. Therefore you broke the terms of the contract. You got no case, so go on 'bout your business!"

And the devil, seeing that he was outsmarted, started to rant and rave and curse and swear as he stormed out of the house 'cause he never thought any human could have tricked him like that.

Good for Chris he had such a wife who was very wise to have thought about Daylight Savings Time.

## The Bus

A group of passengers were traveling in a bus on a highway through a barren, desolate countryside late in the evening, after dark; and, as they seemingly sped along at the speed permitted in that region, for a very long while, no one said a word or made a sound. They were all sitting quietly, sleeping, or thinking, or gazing out into the darkness. The bus must have been traveling for hours and hours until, finally, one man spoke. He had been sitting quietly, wide awake, for a very long time, but now he could hold it in no longer.

"What are we doing here?" he asked. "Will someone please tell me what we are doing here, and why, for God's sake, are we on this bus?"

He paused, with his eyes wide open, mouth gaping as if expecting an answer; but everyone just looked at him in a rather strange way.

He continued, "What madness is this? Doesn't anybody know why we are here?" Then he turned to one of the other passengers, an old man, and said, "You, sir, would you tell me what you are doing on this bus?"

"Why...,why...,I...,I..." replied the old man.

"See what I mean—he doesn't know why he is here! Can't somebody give me a sensible answer?" Turning to a younger man, he said, "You, young man with the earphone stuck in your ears, what are you doing on this bus?"

"What you say? You talking to me—you talking to me, man?"

"Yes, I'm talking to you! I said, why are you on this bus, and where are you going?"

"Well, now, the fact that I am here and not someplace else, must mean that's the reason, man, and as for the second question, I got to be going someplace 'cause we ain't standing still, are we?"

"There is another example! All doubletalk, but he doesn't know from A to Z what he is doing here. I doubt that he even knows who he is, or where he is, much less why he is here!"

189

Suddenly another passenger, a young lady, spoke up. "Why are you asking us these questions, anyway? Why don't you ask yourself why you are here? Tell us why you are here!"

"Why would I be asking a question if I knew the answer?" he said to her.

"What! Didn't you know when you first got on the bus what you were getting on the bus for, and where you were going?"

"You think you're smart, don't you!" he replied. "Well, then tell me, did you see me get on this bus? Did you see anybody else, for that matter, get on this bus? Can you tell me where you got on the bus? I bet you can't even tell me that!"

"What a silly thing to say! Why sure I can! I..., I..., I..." And without finishing her sentence, she sat down and didn't say another word.

At that moment, a man who said he was a retired lawyer made the following remark. "Why is it important to know why we are here? Would it make any difference? Would it change anything?"

"Why is it important? Of course it is important," said the first man. "If we don't know why any of us is here, then we might as well not exist, because you, me, none of us would have any meaning or purpose!"

"That's just the point," said the lawyer. "Maybe we don't! For all we know, we don't even exist! Maybe we are just a weird dream in somebody's head and aren't even real! As soon as the dreamer awakens, poof, all our troubles will be over!"

"I wish it were as simple as that, really, I do! But if that were true, we would have no past or future, nor substance! Yet I know I have a past! I am somebody! I can feel! I can think!"

"All right, you are somebody, and you have a past. Then what was the last thing you were doing before you found yourself on this bus, or even yesterday, or the day before for that matter? Just where were you? And what were you doing? That is your past, isn't it? So tell us what you remember!"

"That's easy—let me think! Let me think! I remember I...I remember I was... I was...What the hell's happening to me? I can't even remember where I was or what I was doing before I got on the bus!"

At this point, an elderly lady said to him, "Young man, why do you torture yourself like that? Why don't you take it easy and stop thinking so much? Sooner or later, it all has to come to an end. It's no use to worry! Sit down and enjoy the ride!"

Then a white-goateed, bespectacled man, a professor who was sitting at the back of the bus listening to everything, called out and said, "Wait a minute—maybe I can solve this mystery! I have a theory as to why we are here! Have you ever heard of mass hypnosis? The reason you can't remember anything, or anybody else can't for that matter, is because we have been hypnotized, all of us! It must be the air we breathed when we entered the bus, or something in the air conditioning that caused it. Look outside. Even though it's dark, all you see is the shadows of trees and open land. I believe we are being taken somewhere against our will—for what purpose, I don't know!"

What the professor said disturbed everyone and almost started a pandemonium until the first man calmed them down. "What are you trying to do, cause a panic? Are you trying to get us all killed? Calm down! I think we should ask the bus driver where we are going before we all get excited!"

Just then someone said, "Quiet, everybody! Quiet! Listen to what the driver is saying over the CB. They talk to each other all the time, you know, these bus drivers!" Then everybody was quiet as they listened.

"Hey, Mac! How's it on your end, buddy!" said one chauffeur.

"Everything is fine! Road's wide open—ain't nothing moving as far as the eyes can see. What's your cargo tonight, Billy Boy! What you got?"

"Oh, I got about forty or so, not a bad load at that, but they're acting a bit restless right now. How about you? What you got, Mac?"

"'Bout the same as you, Billy Boy! Looking forward to some hot coffee and chow! Ten-four, Billy Boy!"

"Ten-four, Mac! See you later!"

"See what I told you," said the first man. "The driver knows where we're going!"

"Yeah, ask him, ask him!" they all said in unison.

The first man approached the driver. "Billy Boy, where you taking us? We all would like to know where you taking us?"

"What you mean, where I'm taking you? Every last one of you bought a ticket that says where you're going. Look on your ticket receipts, and don't be bugging me, before you make me wreck this bus!"

They all looked for their ticket receipts, searching in their pockets, their wallets, their pocketbooks, but nobody could find a receipt. That was strange! Very strange, they thought!

So the first man went back to the driver and said, "Look, Bill Boy, something strange is going on here—nobody can't seem to find their receipt!"

"Well, I ain't got nothing to do with that. All I know is I didn't let nobody on my bus unless they had a ticket!"

"Yeah," said the first man, "well if that's the case, then you got all the tickets or stubs! Where are the tickets you collected? Show them to us!"

"Where the what? Where the what? What tickets? What stubs? What you talking about?" Then he paused and said, "Come to think of it,...you're right,...I should, .. but I don't! I mean...I mean...Maybe you...better sit down...When you get to...terminal...ask all the questions... you like...don't know...don't know...I...I..."

So the first man went back and told the people, "The bus driver is crazy! He don't know any more than we do! We got one of two choices, we can wreck the bus—cause he's not stopping no matter what we say—or we can wait until we reach wherever we're going and speak to the management. Somebody will have to give us an explanation one way or the other!"

Most of them thought that was a good idea, but one woman said, "Wait a minute, now! That means you think the professor is right! But what if he's wrong, and we are not hypnotized as he said. After all, I never heard of air in a bus or air conditioning hypnotizing people. That's not how people are hypnotized at all! And I don't buy the other theory about being in somebody's dream, either!"

"Then what is your theory? Do you have one?" asked the first man.

"Well," she said, "look at it this way. We are all on the bus, and we don't know why we're here or where we are going. We don't know how we got on the bus. People are not apt to forget such things. This is not real—although some people would say, how do we know anything is real, and that we have been walking around in a dream all our lives anyway, making up things and calling it real, or they might say, it's just as well we don't remember what never existed. But I'm not into metaphysics!"

"Yeah, well get to the point! What is your theory?" they demanded of her.

"All right, this is what I think. I think we are all dead! In another dimension, in limbo somewhere, and we've lost all past consciousness! I think it wouldn't matter if we jumped off this bus, or ran it off a cliff, or put a bullet in our heads, we can't die 'cause we're already dead! We are all lost souls in purgatory!"

"Well," said the first man, "that's a fine theory, but nobody's going to test it, 'cause I am sure not going to jump off this bus or shoot myself to find out. You, Ms. Smarty, you jump off and anybody else with you! Anyone else has any more theories or bright ideas?"

No one answered, and they all started to look at him again in a rather strange way, as, one by one, they resumed sitting quietly, sleeping, or thinking or gazing out into the darkness as the bus seemed to speed on its journey on a lonely highway in a lonely countryside. The first man, too, finally became weary, and he, too, at last sat down quietly, wide awake, staring into nowhere!

Before you knew it, it was daybreak, and daylight shone through the windows, and sounds of laughter came from very close by. You could hear the happy voice of a boy and that of an older person, perhaps his father, who said to him, to the boy's delight, "All right, son, you have permission! You can go ahead, but breakfast will soon be ready!" And the boy burst into the room where there was a huge model of a country landscape and highways and hills, and little toy Greyhound buses with toy people inside. It was a model he and his father had put together several days ago. There was one toy bus that seemed to have fallen into a ravine and capsized. The boy carefully picked it up and set it on the highway again, pointing north, and he carefully picked up the first man, the professor, the young woman, the retired lawyer, the old man, each little toy person, and carefully set them in their seats again in their imaginary and unreal world, but a world nevertheless that brought so much joy to one happy little boy!

## About the Author

John Weldon Evans was born in La Boca, Canal Zone and attended La Boca Elementary, Junior High, and Normal Training School during the nineteen thirties and forties. He taught in the Canal Zone "colored schools" in the towns of Silver City and La Boca, C.Z. until the year 1956 when he, like many other Canal Zone youths, left to further their education and careers in the U.S.A. In the U.S., he achieved a B.A. and two M.A. degrees, and worked as a lecturer, and later an administrator at the State University of New York Manhattan Educational Opportunity Center, where he is currently serving as Associate Director in charge of Academic Affairs.